THE
Black BOOK
OF
BOUNDARIES

ONYX EDITION

TIFFANY BUCKNER

© 2021, Tiffany Buckner
The Black Book of Boundaries
www.tiffanybuckner.com
info@anointedfire.com

Published by:
Anointed Fire™ House
www.anointedfirehouse.com

Cover Design by:
Anointed Fire™ House

Author photograph by:
Photo by: Brand You Brand Nu

Edited by:
Jose Juguna

ISBN: 978-1-7354654-6-3

Note from the Author

Hey you! Thank you for purchasing the Book of Boundaries (Onyx edition). Before you move any further into this book series, I want to share my heart with you regarding this series. After having ministered to or counseled countless women about boundary-setting, I came to realize more and more that the issues that are ever-so-prevalent in this world are mainly centered around a need for boundaries. I can truly say that more than ninety percent of the people I've coached, counseled or mentored were in dire straits simply because they didn't have any solid or healthy boundaries set in their lives. In truth, most people have never had anyone to teach them how to properly set boundaries. Consequently, our mental institutions and prisons are overflowing with people whose minds have been overtaken by the enemy. All the same, school shootings, racism, divorce, rape, abuse and every evil thing in the Earth has been thriving as the human race continues to descend into madness. This is why I created the Book of Boundaries!

You'll notice that there are five parts to this series. They are:
1. **The Onyx Edition** (You are here)
2. The Emerald Edition
3. The Sapphire Edition
4. The Jasper Edition
5. The Ruby Edition

I chose these names for several reasons, but mainly

because of what those colors represent. All the same, each of these stones could be found in the ephod of the high priest. "Ye have seen what I did unto the Egyptians, and how I bare you on eagles' wings, and brought you unto myself. Now therefore, if ye will obey my voice indeed, and keep my covenant, then ye shall be a peculiar treasure unto me above all people: for all the earth is mine: And ye shall be unto me a <u>kingdom of priests</u>, and an holy nation. These are the words which thou shalt speak unto the children of Israel" (Exodus 19:4-6). Believers are priests or priestesses of the Most High God, and as such, we should not be in bondage to any person or system that is contrary to our design! This means that these books are all about IDENTITY! They will help you to better understand who you are, and give you the confidence needed to embrace your God-given identity! Once you do this, it will be easier for you to appreciate yourself enough to establish boundaries.

Each of these books represent your exodus from one mindset to another one. You won't just learn about boundaries, but you will learn a lot about yourself while reading this series! You will learn about demonology, relationships and how the enemy advances against the minds of God's people by simply using the technology of ignorance! You will go from black to blue, from not knowing to understanding why it is necessary for you to set boundaries, what it looks and feels like to live behind boundaries, and what you stand to gain once you effectively set and enforce boundaries in your life. You will learn about the infamous narcissist and how to rid your life of that evil force once and for all. This is a must-have book for the sane and the insane! It is designed to help you to take back the real estate of your mind that the enemy has stolen from you!

In this series, I also shared some of my personal stories and dreams with you so that you can also witness the exodus that I had to take from being a mess to a living message! I shared these stories so that you can know that it is POSSIBLE for you to completely leave and annihilate one mindset and lifestyle, and wholeheartedly embrace another reality that looks NOTHING like the one you left behind!

Welcome to the Book of Boundaries! Warning: revelation produces a paradigmatic shift, which causes things in your life that shouldn't be there to wither up and fall away. In other words, if you like being broken, bound and miserable, don't go any further because the revelation in this series is potent enough to sober you up! But if you're ready for a change, flip the page!

Sincerely,
Tiffany Buckner

Introduction

Scriptures for this edition

In the beginning was the Word, and the Word was with God, and the Word was God. The same was in the beginning with God. All things were made by him; and without him was not any thing made that was made. In him was life; and the life was the light of men. And the light shineth in darkness; and the darkness comprehended it not.
John 1:1-5

In the beginning God created the heaven and the earth. And the earth was without form, and void; and darkness *was* upon the face of the deep. And the Spirit of God moved upon the face of the waters.
Genesis 1:1-2

The onyx stone is Black.

The color black, in this edition, represents a void or lack of revelation. We all have voids in certain areas of our lives; these are the black spots on our souls, and for the most part, the average person does not have any measure of revelation as it relates to boundary-setting. The color black, in this edition, simply represents the temperature that readers start off with. The goal is to grow the reader from cold to hot, meaning each reader will start off with the information that he or she came with, but as readers navigate through this book, they will become smarter, wiser and more confident. When God created Heaven and Earth, the first thing He noticed was that the Earth was without form and void; what shaped the Earth was the movement of God upon the waters. God then said, "Let there be revelation," or as we've read it, "Let there be light." When the light came on, the water turned from black (cold and void) to blue (warm and full of life); it was so pure that on the fifth day, He began to populate it with fish and the many fascinating creatures that are housed in the seas, oceans, rivers and lakes that fill our Earth.

The goal is to grow you, the reader, from cold to hot in the area of boundary setting and as it relates to life in general. You will find that this book is information-rich; it is filled with revelation that you can apply to every area of your life. You will learn how to set mental boundaries, physical boundaries and spiritual boundaries.

TABLE OF CONTENTS

UNDERSTANDING BOUNDARIES

"Our Father which art in heaven, hallowed be thy name
Thy kingdom come. Thy will be done in earth, as it is in
heaven
Give us this day our daily bread
And forgive us our debts, as we forgive our debtors
And lead us not into temptation, but deliver us from evil: For
thine is the kingdom, and the power, and the glory, for ever.
Amen. For if ye forgive men their trespasses, your heavenly
Father will also forgive you: But if ye forgive not men their
trespasses, neither will your Father forgive your trespasses."
(Matthew 6:9-15)

Most, if not all, of us are familiar with the Lord's prayer.
We've used this prayer as a template for thousands of years,
quoting it both religiously and intimately. Howbeit, one of the
words that sticks out in this prayer is "trespass." What does it
mean to trespass, and why is it so important to God that we
forgive everyone who does it? To get a better understanding,
let's first look at the definition and the history of the word
"trespass."

Trespass:
- enter the owner's land or property without permission
  (Google Online Dictionary).
- an unlawful act committed on the person, property, or
  rights of another especially: a wrongful entry on real

property (Merriam Webster).
- to encroach on a person's privacy, time, etc.; infringe (Dictionary.com).
- To pass over, to go beyond one's right in place or act; to injure another; to do that which annoys or inconveniences another; any violation of law, civil or moral; it may relate to a person, a community, or the state, or to offenses against God. The Hebrew 'asham ("sin"), is used very frequently in the Old Testament when the trespass is a violation of law of which God is the author. The Greek word is paraptoma (Bible Study Tools).

The word "trespass" is more of a legal term; it denotes the rights, properties and privileges of one party, and the inability for another party to infringe upon those rights. But there would be no trespassing laws if there were no rules or diversity of beliefs. Wherever there are contrasting beliefs, there has to be borders, limitations, restrictions or, better yet, boundaries.

Boundary:
- something that indicates or fixes a limit or extent (Merriam Webster).
- a line that marks the limits of an area; a dividing line (Google Online Dictionary).
- a real or imagined line that marks the edge or limit of something (Cambridge Dictionary).
- The boundary of an area of land is an imaginary line

that separates it from other areas (Collins Dictionary).

A boundary, in short, is a line, either visible or invisible, that marks the end of one thing and the beginning of another; it is a line or space (defined, imagined or assumed) that separates one territory or reality from another. A good example of a defined boundary is a road sign that indicates that you've left one city, county or state, and are entering another. Another great example of a defined boundary are the laws of a region. The majority of citizens in every given region have heard and understand the laws of that region, so a man who decides to rob a bank is intentionally crossing a boundary. The boundary was defined, but he chose to cross it anyhow. Defined boundaries are published; they include laws, company guidelines, contracts and, of course, scriptures. Anyone who decides to cross or violate a defined boundary is a rebel.

An example of an imagined or assumed boundary, on the other hand, is one that is not communicated or one that is presumed. For instance, a man sees a woman at a park. She's attractive and loud, plus, she's wearing a halter top, cutoff jeans and a pair of six-inch stilettos. Of course, she may not want to admit this, but she is communicating with her clothes, however, the question is—what is she communicating and who is she attempting to communicate with? Because of the music he's subjected himself to and the people he's surrounded himself with, he assumes that he can say whatsoever he wants to say to her, so he walks over and says, "Hey gorgeous, can I spend the night with you?" The woman turns and looks at the guy, and she immediately begins to berate and curse at him. Was he being disrespectful? Yes! Did he intentionally cross a boundary? Of course! But his response to her may very well be from his lack of knowledge and his over-exposure to music and a culture that degrades and/or objectifies women. In other words, he's ignorant (and rebellious). The word "ignorant" comes from the root word "ignore." It simply means that information is present, but an individual has chosen not to access that information. We are all ignorant of something. Needless to say, however, this doesn't excuse him, nor does it justify his behavior, but it definitely explains it. You see, the women in his family may be, for lack of a better term, sexually indiscriminate. His mother may have been promiscuous, his sisters may be promiscuous and his father may be in absent figure in his life. So, he's a promiscuous man who's never been truly fathered; he's a man who has been surrounded by sexually immoral people his entire life. For this reason, he has surrounded himself with sexually immoral friends and he listens to music that promotes violence and the sexual objectification of women. So, to him, her choice of clothing communicated that she's promiscuous. But the world or culture she has subjected herself to is a little different; it borders the world or culture that he's been a part of. She grew up in a two-parent home, her mother wasn't promiscuous and her father was an ever-present force in her life. She went to a private school and she listened to a lot of R&B and Pop music. Her choice of clothing has everything to do with the friends she's surrounded herself with, the music she's listened to and the shows she's watched on television. At the same time, her parents never put pressure on her to dress or behave like a self-respecting woman. Instead, they gave her everything she wanted, and they didn't place any boundaries on her because they wanted to give her the "freedom" to make her own choices. In other words, they gave her flesh a free pass. Her reason for dressing the way that she dresses was to compete with her friends, get the attention of a wealthy man in hopes that they'll build a relationship that ends in marriage and to look like her favorite celebrities. As you can see, both parties are subjects of Hollywood culture, however, there are many subcultures in Hollywood that border one another (they are closely related), but the rules and objectives aren't always the same, even though they typically end the same way. Her experiences were different from the experiences of the man who'd approached her, and her expectations didn't match his expectations. Did he know that he'd crossed a boundary? Did he know that approaching her in such a way was disrespectful? Yes, he knew this! But in his world, people cross boundaries all the time, and the people who don't are frowned upon and labeled as weak. In other words, he doesn't respect boundaries; to him, a boundary is a challenge. If he sees something he wants, he's willing to cross a boundary and risk paying the penalty for trespassing in order to get it. Imagined boundaries are oftentimes culturally centered, meaning, they are lines of demarcation that were created by each individual person and are oftentimes a culmination of each person's culture, life experiences and beliefs.

There are eight main types of personal boundaries; they are:
1. Physical
2. Material
3. Legal
4. Mental/Emotional
5. Familial
6. Spiritual
7. Financial
8. Relational

Physical: These are the boundaries we place around our bodies; this includes what we reference as our "personal space" and what we consider to be appropriate versus inappropriate. For example, most churches are extra careful when it comes to their female members and/or visitors; this is especially true for the men on staff. This is because a lot of women have been sexually violated at some point in their lives, so they are very sensitive to the touch of a man. Consequently, if a man decides to pray for them when they are standing at the altar, he has to have another female standing next to him. All the same, he won't touch certain parts of their bodies because doing so could offend, scare and even further traumatize some women. This means that their physical boundaries are different than the boundaries that other women have in place. Most women who are healed don't mind men praying for them and they don't read into every behavior or slip-up, but a woman who hasn't healed has to be handled delicately.

Our clothes are also boundaries that we use to cover ourselves and to protect us from public shame, perversion and/or imprisonment. They form a barrier around us; no one other than our spouses can (legally) walk up to us and lift our shirts. Lastly, physical boundaries include the borders that we place around our bodies when we're courting, for example, when we say that we won't have sex outside of marriage, we are essentially saying that we will not allow someone to tempt us into a sexual relationship as well. These are rules or laws that we establish within ourselves, and every law is not established unless there are penalties to back it and law enforcement to carry it out. This means that if your insignificant other does try to make sexual advances against you, you don't just respond with "no," you also have to warn the person (first offense) and take action against the person (second offense). For example, if I tell a man that I'm abstinent, I expect him to respect this. If he makes sexual advances toward me, I will remind him of my stance and warn him that his behavior will not be tolerated. This is normally enough to end our relationship, but if he sticks around and trespasses again, I would end the relationship because it is then clear to me that he doesn't respect me, my boundaries or my God. It is also clear to me that he has no self-control, and because of this, he wouldn't make a very good husband.

Material: These are the boundaries that we place around our material possessions. For example, I have purses, and I often like to take one of my purses with me whenever I leave my house. No one can go in my purse without my permission. So, if I saw someone with their hand in my purse, I would immediately shove and confront that person. Why? Because there's an invisible boundary around it, one that is culturally understood by everyone in the western world who is three to five years old or older. The walls of our houses form a boundary around our possessions. Our yards form a boundary around our houses.

Legal: The laws of the land form invisible barriers around our homes, our bodies and our possessions. If a stranger walks into our yards, that person could be charged with trespassing; that is, if there is a "No Trespassing" sign in our yards. All the same, if someone stole something from us, manipulated something out of us, withheld something from us or did something to us—if a person has violated any of our boundaries, we can take that person to court. All the same, there are laws of the land that every citizen must abide by; these are the city-issued, state-issued and federal-issued regulations that our government has established.

Mental/Emotional: These are the boundaries that we form around our minds and our emotional health. We do this by:

- **The company we keep:** Most of us intentionally and carefully choose emotionally healthy people to surround ourselves with.

- **Learning to identify and respect seasons:** The truth is that there are some relationships that are seasonal, even though we wish that they were permanent. Identifying when someone's season in our lives has expired (and vice versa) is vital to us maintaining sound minds; this allows us to either transition to another type of relationship with these people or to put a reasonable amount of distance between us. Note: expired seasons don't necessarily mark the end of a friendship; they could simply mean that someone we consider to be our best friend may have to transition into another role, for example, the person may become a distant friend or an associate. Or someone who was just an acquaintance may be suddenly become someone we consider to be a dear or close friend.
- **The boundaries that we place around everything that's important to us:** Undefined boundaries are nothing but electric fences that are not plugged in—they are present, but they have no power. We place boundaries around everything and everyone that we consider to be important.
- **The words we say:** We choose our words carefully, especially with the people we love and want to keep in our lives.
- **The words we accept:** We have the power to accept and/or reject the words spoken over our lives by others. We protect our mental and emotional health by distancing ourselves from people who are mentally,

9

emotionally and verbally abusive.

- **The choices we make:** Every choice we make is tied to our mental and emotional being, so most of us have learned to be careful when making decisions, for example, don't make a rash decision when you're angry, sad or overly excited.

Familial: These are the boundaries that we place around our families. For example, one woman may permit her friends to speak against her family, while another woman wouldn't allow anyone to speak against her family, or there may be limits to what her friends can say. For example, I've had friends who've come from broken, perverted families, and they always spoke negatively about their families. I knew my limits; I could say, for example, that their mothers had a Jezebel spirit or their fathers were terrible fathers, but I could not call someone's mother a whore, regardless of how bad she was. All the same, I could not say to someone that their father was a dumb man, even if he was absent from their lives, and thankfully, I've never even thought of saying these things. But these are boundaries that we sense; they are not always verbally expressed, only sensed. Familial boundaries also involve our spouses and children.

Spiritual: These are the boundaries that we place around our faith. For example, no one can bring a Buddha statue into my home, nor can anyone promote another deity in anything that I publish or host. No one has the freedom to promote their religion in my home, and no one can speak negatively to me about my God. All the same, no one can freely lay hands on me (in prayer) unless I know and trust them; these are spiritual boundaries that again, are culturally understood and not always verbally expressed.

Financial: These are the boundaries that we place around our wealth. For example, no one has the freedom to go into your bank account; that is, unless you give them permission to do so. All the same, no one outside of a spouse has the right to tell you how much money you need to save, spend or invest; they can suggest this, but this is not something they can enforce. Additionally, no one has the right to know how much money you have in your bank account unless you've legally and financially bound yourself to that person or organization.

Relational: These boundaries are similar to familial boundaries, but the difference is, relational boundaries deal with everyone outside of your family unit. For example, your friends and the people you're courting are a part of your relational circle. We pretty much guard our relationships with them by not allowing anyone to speak against them unless they are telling us something to protect our mental, physical, spiritual or financial health. For example, let's say that you're courting a guy and one of your family members see and recognize him. The family member approaches you and says, "Be careful. I know James. He used to date a friend of mine. He pretended to be a holy man of God, got her pregnant, and then, left her for one of her friends." The family member isn't gossiping if she's giving you firsthand information and she's genuinely concerned about your well-being. Nevertheless, if she was just assuming and saying things like, "He has beady eyes. I wouldn't trust him," you may or may not tell her to refrain from speaking negatively about your new beau. This would all depend on how close the two of you are and how much you trust her insight, of course.

It goes without saying that this isn't a complete list of boundary types; these are just some of the main boundaries that we have. Every boundary has a function. The overall goal of a boundary is to protect the integrity of a functioning system. All the same, there are vertical boundaries (thoughts) and horizontal boundaries (actions). A horizontal boundary is a natural boundary; it's the walls that shape our houses, the metal that surrounds our cars and the direction that we travel in at all times. A vertical boundary, in short, is nothing more than a mindset established by a group of beliefs, experiences and doctrines.

There are types of boundaries and there are directions of boundaries. In addition to vertical and horizontal boundaries, there are clear boundaries and then, there are inverted boundaries. Clear boundaries are largely understood because of culture, common practice, religious affiliation, denomination and other variables. These are the boundaries that we don't have to communicate often, but we do have to watch and enforce. Inverted boundaries are personally

established boundaries that we've placed around ourselves and the relationships (personal, organizational) that we are a part of. Some of these borders or limitations do have to be communicated because they are not all societal norms. A great example of an inverted boundary is a boundary established by an unstable couple because one of the partners involved in the relationship is extremely insecure, and the other partner has allowed himself or herself to be limited by the insecure partner. So, if you're a woman and you start talking to a guy about anything from the weather to a problem in the workplace, you may notice that guy looking around for his girlfriend or wife. If he spots her, he'll lower his head and mumble his answer. Noticing his posture, she will make her way towards the two of you and jokingly say something like, "So, what's going on here? Hi, my name is
_____ and I'm his fiancé. Who are you? Do you two know each other?" This is an example of an inverted boundary; it's not normal to see someone behaving like this, so when we do come across odd couples, we often intentionally avoid them because we get tired of unintentionally offending them. Please understand that anytime you cross a boundary, whether it's communicated or not, you are guilty of trespassing, at least, in the other party's eyes. Now, this doesn't mean that you've done something wrong; it could mean that you are unintentionally crossing a boundary that was established outside of normal human reasoning.

Another example worth mentioning is when a single woman

excessively and noticeably tries to avoid engaging in conversation with a married, engaged or unavailable man out of fear that his wife, fiancé or girlfriend will misread her. Women like this have been traumatized at some point by someone who was insecure, so they keep responding to the traumatic event by going out of their way to prove themselves. They'll greet the husbands, but they'll give the wives their undivided attention. They'll help the wives if they need it, but they will avoid the husbands at all costs. They are extremely aware of their surroundings and are known to easily misinterpret certain behaviors. For example, if a single woman attends a gala and comes across the married hosts, she may run around helping the wife with everything, but completely ignore and isolate the husband, and while this is admirable, it can also serve as a red flag to the couple. The single woman may sit at the table with the couple and constantly speak with the wife, ignoring the husband's attempts to have a conversation with her or she may keep her answers short and to the point when responding to him. Let's say that the wife suddenly loses her pep, and it becomes clear that she's ready to go home. Once the couple leaves, the single woman may begin to inwardly panic, thinking that she's said or done something that the wife may have misinterpreted. So, the next time she sees the wife, she will likely approach her and apologize, saying something like, "Hey, I just wanted to apologize for Friday night. When I asked Mr. Barksdale his age, I wasn't trying to be disrespectful, I was genuinely curious because he looks so young." Now, to the single woman, she's proving herself to be a trustworthy woman. But to the married couple, the single woman's behavior is alarming; it signifies that some traumatic event has taken place in her life, and because of that event, she's trying to overcompensate. What she doesn't realize is that she's doing the very thing she's purposed in her heart not to do. Whenever she's around, she's dividing the couple by communicating excessively with the wife, all the while, ignoring the husband. If the couple has employed her to work for them, they may have to either terminate her or move her to a department far away from the husband. Why is this? A traumatized woman misreads just about everything! If the husband says, "Jane, I need to meet with you at two o'clock," she will most likely misinterpret what he's saying. She'll take it to mean that he's flirting with her when he's not. He's simply trying to work with her. So, she may show up at the office with a friend or have the man's wife accompany her into the office. I've actually known women who were wired like this, and they almost always have had to go through deliverance. Their inverted boundaries signaled that something was wrong inwardly. It served as a red flag that something dark was lurking in the woman's heart, and she needed some major healing. Again, inverted boundaries can be either good or bad.

And finally, boundaries have textures, lengths and widths. The three textures of a boundary are:
- **Fluid Boundaries**
- **Solid (Established) Boundaries**
- **Laws**

Fluid Boundaries: These are the boundaries that are flexible, meaning, they have not been solidified. A good example is a woman who declares her abstinence, but when she enters a relationship, she allows her new beau to sleep at her house (or vice versa). She may even allow him to sleep on her bed or on her couch. While she's declared herself to be abstinent, she has no solid boundaries in place to ensure that she remains that way. It is for this reason that the couple will more than likely engage in some form of sexual misconduct with one another. (Please note that non-penetrable sex is still sex, and to Heaven, it is sexual misconduct (fornication), whether it involves masturbation, oral sex or any sexual act or suggestion that is designed to arouse and/or gratify the lusts of one or both of the parties involved.

Solid (Established) Boundaries: Boundaries that are inflexible but can be moved or manipulated whenever the person who's established them is at a crossroads. Established boundaries are relatively solid, but they can be conditional in extenuating circumstances. This is because the person who has established these boundaries is not one hundred percent sure why it was necessary to establish them. The person can be mostly convinced—he or she can be ninety percent sure that a certain boundary is needed, but Satan specializes in the ten percent uncertainty; Satan specializes in doubt. If he sees that there is even a small chance that he can move or remove the borders of a boundary, he is willing to try. God is always trying to get us to completely and wholeheartedly believe Him; this way, we'll learn to establish laws in our lives, and we won't find ourselves falling into sin whenever we're tempted, threatened or provoked.

Laws: These are established boundaries that have no give and no take. A person who has established laws in his or her life has invested time, prayers, energy, sweat, tears and resources into establishing these boundaries. Because of their investment and their time spent in the presence of God, these boundaries have become laws, meaning, any person who violates them will almost always and sometimes immediately be escorted out of the person's life or be penalized in some way or another. A law is an established belief; laws are established when a person wholeheartedly believes, for example, the Word of God, and there is nothing anyone can say or do to move them.

After reviewing the different types and textures of boundaries, take a moment to look at some of the boundaries in your life, especially the ones that have been constantly violated. Ask yourself the following questions regarding each boundary:
1. Are my boundaries defined, imagined or assumed?
2. What are the textures of each of those boundaries?

Be honest with yourself. If you find that you don't have solid boundaries in any of those areas, write down an action plan. Establish new boundaries and every time Satan sends someone to test those boundaries, utilize those moments to test and strengthen your boundaries and your confidence. Keep doing this until they become laws in your life; keep doing this until you become unmovable and unshakable in regard to God's Word.

Note: insecurities are the products of fluid boundaries or boundaries that have been broken repeatedly. If you want to become more secure, you need to solidify your boundaries until they become laws. In the beginning, this may be uncomfortable, but over time, you will come to understand why having and enforcing these boundaries was necessary, and this will help you to build or rebuild your confidence.

THE HISTORY OF BOUNDARIES

The history of a thing helps us to get a glimpse of its future. What you'll come to see is that everything God created, He created with boundaries, including you. Your skin is your natural boundary. Your skin has several functions.

1. Body temperature regulation.
2. It protects your body from the harmful effects of the sun.
3. It serves as a sensory organ, letting you know when something or someone has touched you.
4. It prevents the loss of bodily fluids, and helps you maintain your water and electrolyte balance.
5. Vitamin D synthesis.
6. It protects your body from trauma.

Of course, these are just a few functions of your body's largest organ. In summary, your skin is a boundary and it does exactly what boundaries do—it serves as a protective barrier. Again, everything God created has boundaries. These are the borders or lines of demarcation that separate one kingdom from another.

Genesis 1:1-19: In the beginning God created the heaven and the earth. And the earth was without form, and void; and darkness was upon the face of the deep. And the Spirit of God moved upon the face of the waters. And God said, Let there be light: and there was light. And God saw the light, that it was good: and <u>God divided the light from the darkness</u>. And God called the light Day, and the darkness he called Night. And the evening and the morning were the first day. And God said, Let there be a firmament in the midst of the waters, and <u>let it divide the waters from the waters</u>. And God made the firmament, and divided the waters which were under the firmament from the waters which were above the firmament: and it was so. And God called the firmament Heaven. And the evening and the morning were the second day. And God said, Let the waters under the heaven be gathered together unto one place, and let the dry land appear: and it was so. And God called the dry land Earth; and the gathering together of the waters called he Seas: and God saw that it was good. And God said, Let the earth bring forth grass, the herb yielding seed, and the fruit tree yielding fruit after his kind, whose seed is in itself, upon the earth: and it was so. And the earth brought forth grass, and herb yielding seed after his kind, and the tree yielding fruit, whose seed was in itself, after his kind: and God saw that it was good. And the evening and the morning were the third day. And God said, Let there be lights in the firmament of the heaven <u>to divide the day from the night</u>; and let them be for signs, and for seasons, and for days, and years: And let them be for lights in the firmament of the heaven to give light upon the earth: and it was so. And God made two great lights; the greater light to rule the day, and the lesser light to rule the night: he made the stars also. And God set them in the firmament of the heaven to give light upon the earth, and to rule over the day and over the night, and to divide the light from the darkness: and God saw that it was good. And the evening and the morning were the fourth day.

In the aforementioned scripture, you'll notice that I underlined most of the sentences that mentioned the word "divide." There are several Greek words used to reference the word "divide," but "ὀρθοτομέω" (pronounced orthotoméō) is the most accurate in this context. Strong's Greek Concordance defines "ὀρθοτομέω" as: to make a straight cut, i.e. (figuratively) to dissect (expound) correctly (the divine message):—rightly divide. In short, God cut out and assigned each part of the Earth a function. The rules or borders that He placed on each function are called boundaries. Every time God "divided" something, He gave that thing its unique function; it could not function in any other way other than the way He assigned it to function, after all, His Word cannot and will never return to Him void. He created the Earth and then, He divided it into sections. One section is called the sky (heavens), the other section is called the ground (earth) and the other section is called the waters (oceans, seas, lakes, rivers). After He was finished doing this, He gave each section a function or an assignment. And finally, He began to fill each dimension of the Earth with living things. This is because, in order for each dimension of the Earth to function, it needs life to sustain; this is because that same life also sustains it. The dependency of two or more organisms on one another to complete a function is called a system.

To get a better understanding of how a system functions, think of the gears, levers and wheels of a machine. The machine in question has to be powered up to work, and only something or someone who has power can power it up. Once the machine is plugged in and powered on, the gears begin to turn. In order for the machine to function, some of the wheels have to move in the same direction (agreement) and some have to move contrary to one another (disagreement). Without agreement, some machines would malfunction because one set of the gears would turn clockwise, while others are turning counterclockwise. This would cause the machine to jam and begin to destroy itself. Without disagreement, the gears would lack the power and force needed to perform. This is to say that agreements and disagreements are necessary! So, a company that makes and packages bread will likely have two machines to complete each assignment. One machine would prep the bread, while other machine is designed to package the bread—or the machines can be joined and triggered to work together; this is called a compound machine. Most gears work contrary to one another; this produces more power and causes the machines to function better. Each machine is surrounded by metal; the metal is the skin of the machine. It protects the inner workings of the machine and it regulates the temperature of the machine's interior. This is a picture of a system and how it works.

God created a perfect system; one that mirrored Heaven, but remember what Genesis 1 said of the Earth. There was darkness upon the face of the deep. God is light, so why did He create the night? If you'll reread the passage, you'll notice that darkness already existed before He created light in the realm of the Earth. Darkness was already here; this was a representation of a whole other system that was contrary to the system of the Kingdom of God. Darkness wasn't just an event that took place every 12 hours; it was used to represent a force that was opposite of God. God separated the light of day (good) from the darkness of the night (evil); He placed a limitation on them both, allowing the light to rule the day and the darkness to rule the night. In the King James version of the Bible, the word "darkness" is mentioned 162 times and the word "dark" is mentioned 43 times. In almost every instance where these words are used in the Bible, they are used to symbolize evil. This means that Satan and his angels were already present before God finished designing the Earth. Nevertheless, God did not abandon His project. He wanted to create a space for us. Of course, human logic would cause us to ask the question—why didn't God simply create a separate space for us—one that Satan had absolutely no access to? The short answer is, He did! When He separated the light from the dark, God was drawing boundaries. There was no need to create another Earth for us to dwell in. Just like everything else He'd created, God gave mankind boundaries, but Satan tempted Eve to cross those boundaries. He tempted her to go against the Word of God. Now, human logic (once again) would reason that Eve's offense was minuscule and God's response to it was overkill, but get this—human logic cannot understand, grasp, comprehend or explain the thoughts of the Most High God! His ways are above our ways and His thoughts are above our thoughts. The minute Eve bit into that forbidden fruit, she became a different type of creature. She was no longer just a light (revelation), but she'd become a hybrid. She was now a dwelling place of both light and darkness. She had become the very thing she'd bitten into—forbidden! Led astray and deceived, Eve then convinced her husband to fall into the same trap that she'd fallen into. If he hadn't bitten into the fruit, chances are, they would have experienced the very first divorce ever recorded because again, the minute Eve bit into that fruit, she'd became like the fruit—forbidden! She was defiled, unclean and outside of God's will. So, she seduced Adam outside the will of God; this is what allowed their marriage to stay intact. The two had crossed a boundary, and because of this, they could no longer live in a place of perfection; they could no longer live in the Garden of Eden. God then expelled the couple from the Garden; they were no longer allowed to cross the border between their new reality and their former reality. Because He'd created man in His image, He'd also given us the freedom to exercise our own will. Darkness and light cannot coexist; they cannot rule together! They are from two different systems! The wheels (or wills) spin in opposing directions, meaning, they clash! Once darkness entered the heart of man, God knew that mankind would continue to rebel against Him. He knew that, if given the chance, we'd try to reenter the Garden of Eden without His permission. Genesis 3:22-24 reads, "And the LORD God said, Behold, the man is become as one of us, to know good and evil: and now, lest he put forth his hand, and take also of the tree of life, and eat, and live for ever: Therefore the LORD God sent him forth from the garden of Eden, to till the ground from whence he was taken. So he drove out the man; and he placed at the east of the garden of Eden Cherubims, and a flaming sword which turned every way, to keep the way of the tree of life."

Adam and Eve went on to birth three sons: Cain, Abel and Seth. Of course, we all know the story. Before Seth came into the Earth, Abel had been murdered by his brother, Cain, because of Cain's jealousy. God accepted Abel's offering, but He'd rejected Cain's offering. Cain allowed bitterness to enter his heart and, as a result, he slew his brother. Amazingly enough, this was the very reason mankind it had been necessary for man to be escorted out of and banned from the Garden of Eden the minute mankind fell. When Satan approached Eve in the Garden, he set out to deceive her because he was jealous of her and her husband's position. He was jealous of their relationship with God. And while there were no Ten Commandments at that time, what Cain had done was still a sin. How so? Because it did not reflect the character and/or heart of God; it reflected darkness—the very forces God had separated from Himself. God is Love (see 1 John 3:8), but hatred is a work of darkness.

Some time later, Noah entered the Earth. He grew to be a

man of integrity, a true man of God, even though he was surrounded by evil on every side. God decided to destroy the Earth with a flood, but He wanted to preserve the light that was Noah. The Lord gave Noah a set of instructions, and being the integral man that he was, Noah obeyed the voice of God. He built the ark and brought his family into the huge structure with him. This is when God caused it to rain upon the Earth for forty days and forty nights. He allowed the waters, which had once been given boundaries, to roam freely. Consequently, all of mankind was destroyed, save Noah and his family. The waters invaded the skies and the land. Without boundaries, water was no longer just another resource; it became a graveyard for many. Eventually, most of the waters evaporated, and the rest of the waters withdrew back to the boundaries that God had originally established for them. Noah and his family left the ark, and over the course of time, sin began to manifest its ugly head once again.

Around sixteen hundred years later, another patriarch was born. God was still interested in establishing boundaries with His people and trying to get them to understand the importance of separating themselves from their lustful desires. So, He met with Moses on Mount Sinai and gave him what we'd come to call the Ten Commandments.
1. You shall have no other gods before Me.
2. You shall not make idols.
3. You shall not take the name of the LORD your God in vain.

4. Remember the Sabbath day, to keep it holy.
5. Honor your father and your mother.
6. You shall not murder.
7. You shall not commit adultery.
8. You shall not steal.
9. You shall not bear false witness against your neighbor.
10. You shall not covet.

These are all boundaries! What God was saying to His people is to abide in His will, and to avoid venturing off into the many traps of sin. And if you want to summarize all of these commandments, what God was really saying is, "Love me and love your neighbor as you love yourself." These are the two commandments that Jesus gave us, but He also mentioned that He hadn't come to abolish the law, but to fulfill them. To fulfill means to complete. We are no longer under the Mosaic Law, however, we are still commanded to love God with everything in us and to love one another. In other words, it's still not okay for us to have idols, kill one another, envy one another and so on. So, if a man steals, his sin isn't that he stole something, his sin is that he didn't know God enough to love and trust Him to provide for him. So, his sin is found in his lack of love and not his abundance of error. The transgression, on the other hand, is the act itself!

As time continued to unfold, the rebellion of man's heart, coupled with the presence of dark forces led this Earth to be in the state that it's in today. From the beginning of time, God has been creating boundaries and systems, and ever since mankind fell from grace, we've been violating those boundaries and perverting those systems. The violation of a boundary is called trespassing (sin); the perverting of a system is called rebellion.

God separated the light from the darkness, but mankind managed to become dark creatures. Eventually, the Word wrapped Himself in flesh, came into the realm of the Earth and redeemed us from our sins using His own blood. And while we are saved from eternal damnation, we are still very much consumers, meaning, we have systems that function sequentially (clockwise) and consequentially (counterclockwise). For example, if I sow into a prophet, the Bible says that I'll reap a prophet's reward; this isn't just a statement, it's a part of the Kingdom's system. So, the minute I sow into a prophet of God, the engine of the Kingdom's system begin revving up and it won't stop until God's Word manifests itself in my life or in the lives of my children. In this, I am flowing in the direction of God's Word; I am in agreement with Him, and therefore, I am walking with Him. "Can two walk together, except they be agreed?" (Amos 3:3) This provokes God's blessings to manifest in my life. It is error and pure deception for us, as believers, to think that we can sow seeds in the devil's system and then reap a harvest from the Kingdom's system. And as asinine as this belief system is, the sad truth is, many believers today are still going into sin looking for blessings, not realizing that sin is a system within itself. If we go into sin, we must expect sin to pay us our wages. It is religious insanity to go into sin, and then look for Heaven to bless us. That's like us working at McDonald's, but expecting Burger King to pay our salary. Again, let's compare a system with the workings of wheels, gears and pulleys! When they all work together, they function in the way they were designed to function, thus allowing them to complete their assignment! The same is true for the will of God! When our wheels (wills) turn in the same direction as God's wheel (will), the will of God begins to manifest itself in our lives. The will of God is the heart of God, from where we'll find everything that we need and want to complete our assignments in the realm of the Earth. When our wheels (wills) turn contrary to God's will, the power of God begins to manifest itself in our lives. The power of God is the Word of God.

Just as Eve bit into the forbidden fruit, we can still sin against God. This is called consequential (counterclockwise); it's what counters God's will and provokes Him to respond. When we move in the opposite direction of God's Word, we simply counter or oppose God's Word or His position. The opposing of God's position or any position is called opposition. It is an opposing thought or action that begins to move up against a functioning system. Now remember, the Word of God cannot and will never return to Him void. Ever! It's impossible for God to lie! This means that whenever our will opposes God's will, our actions provoke God to wrath or, in layman's terms, we tap into His already declared responses to rebellion. He doesn't have to presently address our decisions; He has already spoken, and now, every decision we make either works in agreement with Him or it opposes Him. When your decision opposes the will and the heart of God, it evokes what we call a curse.

- **Blessing:** empowered to prosper
- **Curse:** allowed to fail

The simple truth is you cannot go up against God and win. It's simply impossible! We understand that Hell was not created for mankind; it was created for Satan and his angels. And thankfully, most of us no longer have to worry about spending eternity surrounded by fire and brimstone, however, sin still has a voice in our lives whenever we give it a place in our lives. It still has wages (the produce manufactured by its systems and processes) attached to it, so when a believer submits himself or herself to its system, that believer has to eat the fruit that's produced from that system. Galatians 6:7-8 confirms this. It states, "Be not deceived; God is not mocked: for whatsoever a man soweth, that shall he also reap. For he that soweth to his flesh shall of the flesh reap corruption; but he that soweth to the Spirit shall of the Spirit reap life everlasting." Remember, the Bible was written for the believer, not the unbeliever! I'm saying this because in today's day and age, a lot of people are embracing the ideology of grace being a condom, meaning that believers can now enjoy the perks and the pleasures of a sinful lifestyle without there being any repercussions. I don't think you have to tell any avid Bible reader that this is not true! Whatever a man sows, that he shall also reap!

Grace is the space given for each of us to grow; this space represents time and mercy; this is why in the book of Revelations, Jesus said (of Jezebel), "I gave her space to repent, but she would not." What He was saying is that He extended grace to her, but she took that grace for granted. However, when we are babes in Christ, we are prone to sinful behaviors and God knows this, so He extends grace to us, meaning, He gives us the space to grow. Within the confines or safety of grace, there is a leash or a lease called mercy. I like to think of mercy this way. When we're young in the faith, we tend to go between both systems; we venture between the world's system and the Kingdom's system. When we are in the world's system, we are constantly feeding the appetite of our flesh. Everything you feed grows, but everything you starve has no choice but to die. When we are feeding our flesh, the lust of our flesh continues to grow. Because of this, we find ourselves becoming increasingly darker; our love is confined to a prison that I like to call "conditions," and our flesh is given free roam. The flesh is like a rabid pit bull—it has no loyalty in it. Sure, we could argue that there are folks in the world who are far more loyal than church folks, but I'll venture out to say that this isn't necessarily a truth that we want to lean on, especially when preaching loyalty. People in the world aren't loyal to each other, they are loyal to a set of principles. If you are like me and you grew up in the depths of sin, loving the world and loving rebellion, you should know how hard it is to grow in the midst of the folks you once deemed to be loyal. They won't allow it! They'll allow you to grow a little, but when you start truly serving God and turning away from the old mindset, they will ridicule you, try to sabotage you, try to humiliate you, and some will even try to harm you. This is because breaking up with the old system equates to you breaking up with them in their eyes. What's holding the two of you together is called an agreement; that's it and that's all, but the minute you start falling out of agreement with the old systems, you essentially begin to die your way out of the relationships that you were once a part of. And get this, you're not necessarily rebuking the folks or trying to change them; the problem is, your conversation slowly starts to change, your interests start changing and your circle starts changing. You can have every plan and intention to keep your friends around, but in most cases, they will fall away if you continue to grow. Some do so gracefully, while others do so not-so-gracefully.

EMOTIONAL BOUNDARIES

Have you ever had a point in your life where all of a sudden you found yourself crying a lot? I'm sure we all have. You know that time when you seem to be super-sensitive, and you don't necessarily know why you've been feeling so off? If and when this has happened to you, one of two things was taking place:

1. God made you sensitive to His presence, and not realizing that He wanted to spend time with you, you spent that time watching a bunch of romance comedies and trying to mend broken relationships.
2. Your alarms were going off, indicating that your heart had been hijacked.

Believe it or not, your emotions serve two purposes:

1. **They are doorbells.** They let you know when the enemy is trying to get in, just as they let you know when God is in your midst.
2. **They are alarm systems.** They let you know when the enemy has gotten in, just as they let you know when you are resisting God.

Consider this common scenario. You meet someone who you're romantically interested in. Let's say that he's a guy and you're a girl. (If you're a male, just reverse the order.) Anyhow, the guy calls you on the phone for the first time, and the two of you talk for over an hour. As it turns out, you both have a lot in common. Your new guy-friend invites you out on a date, and you happily accept. Three days later, he picks you up and takes you to a relatively high-end restaurant. While there, the two of you talk for over an hour before the waitress brings your food to the table. Your new friend asks you a few questions, and you answer them all eloquently and without hesitation. You share a lot of your life's stories with the guy, and he listens intently. You notice how engaged he is with you when you speak, and how attentive he is to every word that you utter. He shares a few details about himself, some of which are relatively "sensitive information," meaning that the timing was too soon for him to share that level of information, nevertheless, he explains why he's shared this info with you. He says, "I don't know why, but I feel extremely comfortable with you. It's almost as if I've known you for a long time." In that moment, you can relate to him because there is some level of familiarity present amongst the two of you. And just when you thought that your connection with him couldn't get any stronger, he stretches out his right hand and subtly places it on top of your hand. Your eyes meet, and he says to you, "I really, really like you."

Later that evening, he takes you home and the two of you elect not to share your first kiss just yet. Howbeit, you do sit in his car for two hours, talking all the more about your dreams, your pasts, and your plans for the future. Around eleven o'clock, he walks you to your front door, and the two of you feel an extreme connection. You want to kiss him and he wants to kiss you, but you both resist the temptation to do so, electing to hug one another instead. Once you're in the house, you find yourself immediately reminiscing about the beautiful night you shared with this guy. It's all happening so fast, but you don't want to stop it because it feels so amazingly good to have such an intimate connection with another human being.

He texts you to let you know he's arrived home and tells you how he can't wait to see your beautiful face again. Just seeing his text message causes your heart to skip a beat. The next morning, you wake up to a "good morning" text from him. Every time this guy calls you, you get excited, stop whatever it is that you're doing and rush to answer his call. Your emotions are all over the place, but you're in a happy place, so this doesn't alarm you at all; that is until he neglects to send you a "good morning" text some three days later. As a matter of fact, he doesn't call you like he normally does, and anytime you call him, he doesn't answer his phone. Instead, you have to sit and listen to his annoying voicemail before leaving him a message. All of your text messages are going unanswered. Your heart races from within, your stomach feels like it's twisting in knots and you can barely concentrate. These are all alarm signals going off, signifying that your heart has been hijacked, but get this—these alarms started going off on your first dinner date with the guy. You see, when he started opening up and sharing information with you that was way too intimate for a first date, he was getting you to open your heart; this is the same heart that God told you to guard. Whenever two people engage in a conversation, if one of those people suddenly begins to share intimate details about his or her life, it is human nature for the other party involved to feel obligated to share information that matches or exceeds that level of intimacy. The narcissist knows this, so narcissistic people will tell you things about themselves that they claim no one else knows; this is designed to get you to open your heart and share intimate details with them. This bonding agent speeds up the connection and allows the narcissist to create an emotional soul tie with you within minutes or hours. Some information is valuable; we store it in the vaults of our hearts and we only share it with the people who are the most valuable to us. But a narcissist knows how to break open this vault. Your alarm went off the minute you felt what we often describe as "butterflies" in your stomach, a racing heart and sweaty palms. Nevertheless, you didn't realize that this was an alarm initially because somehow, like most westerners, you came to believe that those feelings were just indicators that you were falling in love. So, you hit snooze on the alarm until the alarm got louder and more evasive. And now, you find yourself overreacting way too soon simply because you haven't heard from your guy-friend all day long. You begin to revisit conversations you've had, looking for clues as to why he seems to be avoiding your calls. You mentally sort through your last conversation with him, trying to see if you may have said something that offended or hurt him. You stalk his social media pages looking for signs that he's truly avoiding you. The night passes away without you hearing from this guy, and you write this night off as one of the worst nights of your life. In truth, if you don't learn to guard your heart, this night is just a snippet of what is to come.

Around noon the next day, you receive a text message from your guy-friend. "Hello. Sorry about yesterday. I lost my phone and had to go by Sprint to get a new one. Hope you're not mad at me. Call me when you get off from work, beautiful." A wave of relief hits you, and suddenly, you go from being bitter to being chipper. Your emotional alarm system has been going off, but you keep ignoring the sounds of it because you favor the idea that what you have with this guy is special, unique and worth preserving, even though you barely know him. One year later, you have a pending court case and a restraining order against the guy. One year later, you've joined a narcissists help group to better understand what you've just survived.

Love bombing. Every psychologist, psychiatrist, counselor and therapist is familiar with this term. Love bombing is the intentional, strategic and persistent attempt of a person (typically a narcissist) to gain emotional control over another human being by showering that person with gifts, attention and compliments. 1 Peter 5:8 warns us, "Be sober, be vigilant; because your adversary the devil, as a roaring lion, walketh about, seeking whom he may devour." What does it mean to be sober? It means to have a sound mind; it means to not be influenced by any ungodly medium, whether that be alcohol, a human being, wealth, fear or a demonic entity. When we hear the word "sober," we automatically think about alcohol and its effects. We automatically think about intoxication versus sobriety. And this is a great picture to consider when trying to understand what God meant when He told us to be sober-minded. Please understand that the narcissist wants to get you under his (or her) influence. When a person is intoxicated, we say that the individual is under the influence, right? What we mean is that the person's logic has been hijacked by alcohol or whatever it is that is influencing the person. We can go under the influence of just about anything! This is why God told us to guard our hearts! But anytime you come in contact with someone who has ungodly motives or someone who has never learned to court outside of a demonic system, that person is going to look for ways to circumvent whatever boundaries you have in place. I've seen women, both Christian and non-Christian, using demonic practices to ensnare men … out in the open! A woman can stand inside of a church, stare a married man in the eyes and utilize her words, facial expressions and movements to ensnare him. Ask any woman and she will tell you that she's seen this a thousand times over! What she's doing is bringing that man under her influence! What this means is, she's creating a moment or a snapshot for him to take home with him. If he's married, he may find himself lying next to his wife, unable to stop thinking about that moment! The more he thinks about her, the more intoxicated or bewitched he'll be by her. Before long, he'll find himself unable to stop thinking about her, and anytime he begins to sober up, that woman will search him out and strengthen her hold on him. She may do this by lightly touching his chest, asking him for advice (men are naturally drawn to damsels in distress) or by outright flirting with him. This doesn't mean that she wants him; she simply wants him to want her! But this behavior can be curved or even stopped if he responds correctly. If he draws boundaries around himself and his marriage, that woman (and everything in her) will be rendered powerless. If he refuses to gaze into her eyes when she tries to stare him down, if he tells her not to touch him when she reaches for his jacket or if he reminds her that he is married when she begins to flirt, she will eventually begin to avoid him. This is what I call James 4:7'ing a devil. This makes me think about entrepreneurship. Every time I have a customer who is adamant about not following the posted procedures, but tries to deal with me personally instead of professionally, I know that I'm dealing with a narcissist. It took me years of hardships and headaches to fully learn this lesson. But whenever I enforce my boundaries and adamantly refuse to allow the individual to do business with me his way or her way, the customer then rips off his or her mask and tosses all the niceties out the window. All of the flattery, flirtations and excessive compliments suddenly end! I then see a bunch of not-so-pleasant personalities manifesting. Oftentimes, the individual will fashion himself or herself as a victim and me as a predator, and when this doesn't work, the person begins to behave in a predatory manner. I've been threatened and I've been virtually stalked by some pretty broken individuals, but thankfully, this isn't something that's too frequent. Most of the time, I'm able to diffuse a narcissist and either keep that person from placing an order with me, or I'll get that person to respect my procedures and policies by telling him or her about the extra fees associated with the extra work he or she is inquiring about. In other words, if he or she wants more of my time, that person has to pay more money, and this is oftentimes effective because narcissistic people love imbalance. They have to absolutely feel in control; they hate or, better yet, abhor, detest and loathe feeling helpless. So, they have to create an imbalance where others are more indebted to them than they are to those people; this allows them to have some measure of leverage in any and every given relationship, whether it be platonic, familial, professional or religious. In the secular world, they refer to people like this as narcissists, but in the church, we call this personality the Jezebel spirit. And without going into any demonology teachings, what I can say is this—the most common hijacker of the heart is the narcissist/Jezebel personality. And anytime the heart has been hijacked, it responds through our emotions. This is why you may find yourself waking up and feeling super emotional all of a sudden. If and when this happens, look at every relationship, especially the intimate ones, and examine each one of them using the Word of God as your guide. If you find a broken or narcissistic individual too close to your heart, you've found the reason that your alarm is going off.

Everything God created, He created in order. My pastor (Apostle Bryan Meadows) teaches about the garden versus the wilderness. He often teaches that:
1. the garden is a place of order.
2. the wilderness is a place of disorder.
3. When God created Adam and Eve, He placed them in the Garden of Eden (a place of order).

In a garden, everything has to be cultivated; every plant grouping has a section to call its own. Gardens are beautiful to behold; they should be pruned, watered and maintained daily. Gardens need the loving touch of humans. Nevertheless, in the wilderness, there is no order. Plants and trees drop their seeds, and those seeds are often caught up by the winds and blown all over the place. They fall to the ground and begin to grow roots. There is no order, no pruning and no maintenance taking place in a wilderness. Consequently, weeds grow amongst the flowers, insects attack plants at will and disease is commonplace. All the same, in the wilderness, there are wild animals at large. In the wilderness, the general mindset is kill or be killed; every animal operates under what I like to call a "survivor's mindset." The same is true for broken and narcissistic people. In most cases, they've been raised in environments where there was no order. In short, there was no structure in their homes, and all too often, their parents behaved like wild animals. In other words, they were raised in the wilderness. It is no wonder that they hate order, structure, processes, protocol, systems and procedures. They want to do any and everything off the radar; this is why God gave us a set of rules that are guaranteed to guard us against people like this. Those rules, of course, are outlined in His Word! Those rules teach us to live in the garden (the place of order) and refuse to go into the wilderness to court, entertain, marry or rescue a person who, quite frankly, doesn't want to be saved. This is no different than taking a tiger out of its natural habitat and tossing it into a cage; it's cruel to the tiger, even though it's entertaining to onlookers. And again, anytime someone comes close to your heart who hates order, the alarms that are your emotions will begin to sound off. Don't think that every pleasant emotion is indicative of a pleasant event taking place; it is normally you misinterpreting the sound of the alarm simply because your belief system has been hijacked. You believe that you're in love; you believe that the other person is in love with you. But when God said for you to guard your heart, He was telling you to guard your belief system. This way, you can effectively test any and every spirit that auditions for a role in your life. If you don't allow your heart or your emotions to be hijacked, you can remain logical, and this is what will allow you to soberly examine the person who's attempting to court or befriend you. Narcissists won't stick around for the entirety of this examination because they want to create soul ties as fast as they can. When they're not allowed to love bomb you, they'll oftentimes start convincing themselves that you are mishandling them, and consequently, they'll go away. This is what you want! This is what it means to James four-seven the devil!

If you want to live a life of peace and prosperity, you have to create boundaries around your emotions. You have to be willing to scare off people who hate order; these are the people who'll have you convinced that you can go into sin and come out with someone other than a sinner. These are the people who'll have you convinced that if you dig long enough, cry hard enough or pray loud enough that you'll eventually pull a blessing out of perversion. And of course, perversion isn't always sexual; it means that an object or a person is not functioning the way it, he or she was designed to function. God didn't design us to sin against Him. In summary, you simply won't pull a good thing out of the wilderness. Even if you give it a name, put a bow on its head and teach it to sit, a wild animal will remain just that—a wild animal!

Matthew 7:16-20: Ye shall know them by their fruits. Do men gather grapes of thorns, or figs of thistles? Even so every good tree bringeth forth good fruit; but a corrupt tree bringeth forth evil fruit. A good tree cannot bring forth evil fruit, neither *can* a corrupt tree bring forth good fruit. Every tree that bringeth not forth good fruit is hewn down, and cast into the fire. Wherefore by their fruits ye shall know them.

Matthew 12:33: Either make the tree good, and his fruit good; or else make the tree corrupt, and his fruit corrupt: for the tree is known by his fruit.

Galatians 5:19-24: Now the works of the flesh are manifest, which are these; Adultery, fornication, uncleanness, lasciviousness, idolatry, witchcraft, hatred, variance, emulations, wrath, strife, seditions, heresies, envyings, murders, drunkenness, revellings, and such like: of the which I tell you before, as I have also told you in time past, that they which do such things shall not inherit the kingdom of God. But the fruit of the Spirit is love, joy, peace, longsuffering, gentleness, goodness, faith, meekness, temperance: against such there is no law. And they that are Christ's have crucified the flesh with the affections and lusts.

PHYSICAL BOUNDARIES

Romans 12:1 is probably my favorite scripture, as weird as that sounds. It reads, "I beseech you therefore, brethren, by the mercies of God, that ye present your bodies a living sacrifice, holy, acceptable unto God, which is your reasonable service." I think it's one of my favorites because this was the area that I needed the most help. No one ever drew boundaries around me physically or mentally, so I didn't know how to draw boundaries around myself. That's a strong statement to make, but it's the reality for so many people. We didn't choose our testimonies; we simply survived them.

I found myself getting in on the passenger's side of an ex's vehicle. It wasn't really his, per se; the vehicle belonged to his stepfather. It was an old pickup truck, and I had an uneasy feeling about getting in it because I'd broken up with the guy a week prior to this incident and he'd randomly shown up at my house after I'd refused to take any of his calls. I'd repeatedly said "no" to the idea of us going outside to talk, but after listening to him and my little sister put pressure on me, I finally gave in. My sister believed him when he said that he only wanted to talk. I eventually reasoned within my heart that I could convince him once and for all that we simply could not be together. I knew that there was no way I was going to reconcile with him; I didn't have even a twinkling of a desire to "fix things." Once we were outside, he suggested that we go and sit in the truck. At first, I said "no," but after a few minutes, I reluctantly agreed. He opened the passenger's side door for me, and I got in. I felt incredibly uneasy, but I ignored all of the alarms that were going off in my head. I was in "survivor's mode" so I immediately started scanning the truck to ensure that I'd be safe, but just as the door was closing, I noticed that the interior door handle was gone. Nevertheless, it was too late. Before I could respond, the door closed, and there was no way that I could get out of it without his help ... or so I thought. He got in the truck and sat there behind the steering wheel a few seconds before saying anything. "I love you, Tiffany." I don't remember most of what he'd said that day, but I do remember that our conversation took a dark turn when I made it clear that I did not want to reconcile. I suggested that we be friends, but after a few "I love you's," from him, followed by a stream of tears, he turned on the truck's ignition. I remember the last thing he said before he pulled off. He said, "I love you and I'm not gonna let you leave me!" And then, off we went. "What are you doing?!" I asked him. But he wouldn't respond to any of my questions. He just kept driving with one hand and hitting the steering wheel with the other hand, and shouting, "I'm not gonna let you leave me like that! I love you! I'm not gonna let you leave me!" Again, I was in survivor's mode, meaning, I became super alert and calm. I started looking around for a way out of the truck. I knew that this guy was about to drive me to his home town, which was 45 minutes away. My Mom didn't know his address, nor did any of my friends. I knew that if he was successful in kidnapping me, he would have held me against my will because of how I'd broken up with him. You see, I'd ended our relationship after he'd gotten upset with me while I was visiting him. He'd made a few comments about how his friend had managed to "tame" his girlfriend and had successfully gotten her to stop wearing them "ho" clothes (slang for whore). I'd angered him when I said something to the effect of, "She's better than me! Let a man try that with me and he'd be a history lesson!" Of course, that upset him and he commented, saying that women like me just needed to have someone to knock the fire out of them a few times. Less than an hour earlier, a group of guys had "disrespected" him by hissing at me, and he'd blamed me for the ruckus. The conversation culminated in his house when he'd violently shook me. He'd tried to pretend that he was joking, but I knew he wasn't. I said to him, "Don't shake me like that. You can give me Shaken Baby's Syndrome." He laughed and said, "You're a grown woman! You can't get Shaken Baby's Syndrome!" I countered with, "Yes, an adult can get it. They call it Shaken Baby Syndrome because the majority of victims are babies, but many of the victims are elderly as well. This can cause fluid to build around the person's brain. Shaken Baby's Syndrome is just one of its many names." Before I could finish, he snapped, "Shut up! You think you know everything!" After that, he started going off, saying I was too smart for my own good and how I needed to be humbled. So, I'd elected to leave, but not before ending our relationship. It was foolish to end things while he was so heated, but I'd gotten frustrated and decided to give him a piece of my mind before I left. *Big mistake.* That's when he'd gotten violent, picking me up and throwing me on his bed. He then stood in front of me and pointed his finger at me. "You ain't going nowhere!" he shouted. "Every time you get mad, you want to leave, but I'm not taking it no more! You're going to sit right here, and if you get up off this bed, I'm going to knock you clean out!" I tried getting up a couple of times, but he'd violently shove me back down and then raise his fist. I probably weighed one hundred pounds at the time, so it was pretty easy for him to partner with gravity and toss me back down. Realizing that I couldn't overpower him, I started to cry, but this cry wasn't authentic; it was my attempt to get him to calm down so I could leave. You see, we were both broken and manipulative, but he was the emotional one. I, on the other hand, was the logical one. After he saw me crying, he'd sat down next to me and started apologizing. He then proceeded with his narcissistic attempt to "tame" me by saying, "I love you, but when you wear clothes like that, I feel disrespected." He kept mixing kind words with subtle demands, and I pretended to agree with him. "I have to go for real," I said. "I told my Mom I'd be home by six, plus, I have to work in the morning." After holding me for a few more minutes, he'd asked for a kiss. I knew this was his way of proving to himself that I wasn't mad at him, I was repentant and that all would be well between the two of us. That was the most disgusting kiss I'd ever had to suffer through. Finally, he let me walk out of the house, not realizing that I wanted nothing else to do with him. Now, fast forward to the truck incident. He'd shown up at my house without notice. I'd broken up with him the same day he'd tried to attack me, and after that, I'd refused to take any of his calls. I didn't know that he'd borrow his stepfather's truck, rip the handle off the passenger's side door and make his way to my city, but he did. And now, there I sat on the passenger's side, looking around and trying to figure out how to escape his truck. He finally stopped at a service station, and I saw my opportunity, but I had to wait for him to get out of the truck. He pulled up in front of the gas station and continued to pound on the steering wheel while yelling obscenities at me, and mixing those obscenities with his proclamations of love. I didn't say a word. I just looked out the window, using any opportunity I could to scan the vehicle for an exit. Finally, he calmed down and said, "Now, I'm about to go in and get me something to drink. Do you want anything?" I looked at him and calmly said, "No, I'm not thirsty." Once he got out of the vehicle, I waited for him to enter the store, and that's when I started rolling the windows down. It was an old pickup truck, so I had to manually roll the windows down, and this was no easy task. I remember an older guy walking up to the window and saying, "Baby, are you okay? Do you need me to call the police?" I told him that I was okay and I said "no" to him calling the police; this was because I knew that by the time the cops arrived, I would have been in that truck heading to another city with a psychopath who was hellbent on "taming" me. I also could tell that the older guy would not have been able to protect me from my ex because he was shorter and a little on the heavy side. I elected to run instead. I don't remember if I put my hand out the window or if I asked the guy to open the door; either way, I got out, and immediately started running. I could hear my ex's voice in the distance. "Tiffany!" he shouted in the loudest, most psychotic way that he could. I'm pretty sure people thought that I was either a drug addict or prostitute, but neither were true. I was just a young, foolish woman who didn't know the power of boundaries. He got in his truck and started chasing me, but by the grace of God, he couldn't catch me because every time he pulled up alongside me and stopped the truck, I would run across someone's yard, towards their backyard. He'd then get back in the truck and try to go where he thought I was going so he could cut me off. Eventually, I was able to shake him off my trail, and thankfully, he didn't think to wait at my house for me. Instead, he kept driving around, looking for me. When I arrived home, I beat on the door until my sister opened it. At the same time, my ex was pulling in the driveway as I was banging on the door, and just in the nick of time, I shut and locked the door. After that day, I avoided him at all costs and he eventually stopped calling me.

That was a crazy story, right? How is it that a human being could behave in such a manner? Why didn't he just agree with me that we weren't compatible and just move on with his life? These questions plagued me for years; that is, until I got saved and God helped me to understand the many facets of my life's story. And let me start by saying this—I wasn't a helpless victim. I wasn't predatory either. I was a foolish woman who'd made a lot of mistakes, only to find myself staring down the throats of some of those mistakes. I eventually learned why the Bible tells us:

1. To guard our hearts
2. To abstain from premarital sex
3. To not provoke anyone to wrath

Before we delve into this a little deeper, please look at the spectrum below.

Egypt	Wilderness	Promised Land
Sin	Immaturity	Child of God
Transgression	Double-mindedness	Servant of God
Iniquity	Rebellion	Son of God
Survivor	Overcomer	More than a Conqueror

Egypt represents a kingdom and the Promised Land represents a kingdom. The wilderness is the space or grace between both kingdoms. Both kingdoms are surrounded by lines or, better yet, boundaries. There are two sides to the wilderness; there's the side closest to Egypt; this is the side where new converts can be found. This is also the side where you'll find some believers progressing more and more into sin (rebellion) and outside of the will of God.

Egypt	Wilderness	Promised Land

	Rebellion $\leftrightarrow$ **Deliverance**	

In the wilderness, you'll find people going in cycles, meaning, they are moving, but they are not advancing in God's will. Instead, they are going in circles (this is called religion). You'll find people progressing →forward (this is called relationship), and you'll find people going back ← to what God delivered them from (this is called backsliding). You'll find people who've pitched tents, just as you'll find people who've settled down in the wilderness; they've built their lives in the wilderness, settled down with wild animals and are now producing children in the wilderness.

And then, there's the side where immature children of God stumble around in. The sides that they're on aren't necessarily directional in terms of physicality, but they deal more with the direction that the people are heading in mentally and spiritually. Each person is either advancing in the Kingdom of God or retreating; there is no middle ground. Every person in the wilderness is either moving forward or backwards, and the people who've settled down have essentially retreated to what they know. All of these directions represent mindsets, belief systems and customs. When a man or woman gets saved, that person then enters the wilderness, but that person, at that time, has two identities. In Egypt, he has a name; in the Kingdom, he has a name. His name represents his assignment in both worlds.

When he's in Egypt, he belongs to Pharaoh (the slave master), but if he's saved, he belongs to God, HOWEVER, he has come under the headship or government of Satan. Think of it like this—I'm an American, so I am subject to American laws while I live here in America. If I moved to Asia, Africa or Europe, I would have to follow the laws and customs of the land I live in. If I exercised my American liberties in a country that considered whatever I was doing unlawful, that country would then have the legal right to bind and arrest me. Of course, America can and often does get involved and will try to convince the government of that country to release me or, at minimum, treat me civilly. Nevertheless, America has no jurisdiction on any of these continents, so in the end, the country I was in would decide how they wanted to treat the matter. If they decided to execute me, America would be powerless. If they decided to imprison me for the rest of my life, America would be powerless. If America considered my crime minuscule, they might try to bargain or barter with the country holding me captive; this is especially true if I held a political office or had some type of power in America. America could even threaten to end trade relations or threaten a cold war, but this would only happen if I were an important figure to the country. In the end, I'd likely serve all or the majority of my time in that prison, not because America didn't try to fight for me, but because America (wisely) decided not to directly impact or affect its own economy, or risk the lives of military personnel just to rescue someone who willfully broke the law in another country. This is how kingdom legalities work! I'm a believer; I am a citizen of the Kingdom of God, but if I play around in sin, Satan has the legal right to bind me. This is because the boundaries that surround the Kingdom of God are called faith, but doubt and worry are the boundaries that surround the kingdom of darkness. Here's the thing; we are not redeemed by works, nor are we condemned by them! Nevertheless, our works are a reflection of our trust or distrust for God. For example, if I decide to enter into a relationship with a man, whether that man be saved or unsaved, and we started having premarital sex, it's not the sex that gets me bound. It's the fact that I'm trusting in my own devices to secure my relationship with the man. The sex just further complicates my bondage; it tightens up the soul tie around my heart. This soul tie is called a yoke. Consequently, I'd end up dating, marrying and reproducing with that man outside of God's will. We'd have our wedding in the wilderness; we'd have our children in the wilderness, and we'd likely end up divorcing in the wilderness. Kingdom legalities protect what's behind the borders of the Kingdom, but whatever is done outside of those boundaries, God has already condemned. In other words, what I do with my body is a reflection of what's going on in my mind! The mind enters sin before the body does! This is why the scriptures say in 2 Corinthians 10:5, "Casting down imaginations, and every high thing that exalteth itself against the knowledge of God, and bringing into captivity every thought to the obedience of Christ." Bring those wild thoughts captive! This is also why the Bible says in Matthew 5:28, "But I say unto you, That whosoever looketh on a woman to lust after her hath committed adultery with her already in his heart." The thought precedes the action; the thought is the problem, the action is the fruit or evidence of where the believer stands! So, if I enter sin looking for a blessing, chances are, I'll end up bound! If I settle down in the wilderness, chances are, I'll exchange vows with a wild animal.

Let's revisit the story about me, the angry ex and the battered pickup truck. I wasn't saved at the time (or maybe I was because I did believe in Jesus; I'm just not sure if I'd ever confessed Him as my Lord and Savior). Nevertheless, I was on the wrong side of the spectrum. I was the property of Pharaoh, even though I thought I was my own independent woman (oh how deceived I was). And when I say that I was the property of Pharaoh, I am in NO WAY saying that I belonged to my ex and he could do whatsoever he wanted to do to me. What I am saying is this—I gave my body away in Egypt, and by doing so, I gave the enemy a measure of legality over my body. This is why my ex didn't respect the fact that I no longer wanted to be with him. This is why he drove away with me in his vehicle. It didn't matter that I'd said "no." To him, I was his property. Why? Because I'd had a sexual relationship with him. Sure, no means no and stop means stop, but when we use this argument, for example, to demand our rights as women, we are oftentimes trying to apply a Kingdom legality in a place where boundaries simply do not exist (sin). (Imagine a bunch of folks in hell protesting the harsh conditions). This is the equivalent of me moving to another country, marrying a foreign man and then complaining about his customs. If I want the American way, I'd better stay in America and marry an American. Sure, the law of the land says that kidnapping is a felony; we all know this, but this is a natural law. Howbeit, spiritually speaking, I was a slave to sin, and slaves have little to no rights in sin! Sin is a kingdom, a system and a government all within itself. So while I could have easily had the ex physically arrested, the hard truth is, I was going to keep having to deal with that same spirit in a different body; that is, until I got saved, died my way out of sin and made my way out of the wilderness. Ask any empath how many narcissists he or she has had to deal with over the course of his or her life, and that individual will widen his or her eyes and passionately say, "A lot! I seem to be a magnet for narcissists!" This is because they keep dating the same demon in a different body! This is a spiritual legality; it's not something the American court system (or any physical court system) can preside over. Here's why. The spiritual world is eternal; it outranks the natural world which, of course, is temporal. So, think of it this way. The spiritual world is the Superior Court; the natural world is the District Court. The Superior Court outranks the District Court. So, if you're an empath and you keep attracting narcissists, the most you can do is have those people arrested whenever they break natural laws, but if you stay outside of the will of God, spiritually speaking, that spirit will continue to pursue you. It's a pharaohic spirit that sees you as its property, and no amount of human logic or reasoning will convince it otherwise. I often say this—you can't talk a demon out of being a demon. If you want the benefits of Kingdom laws, you have to navigate to the right side of the spectrum. In other words, you have to draw boundaries around your mind, just as you have to draw boundaries around your body. And get this—I'm not just dealing with sex here! Who you physically avail yourself to, you give a measure of access to. For example, one of the craziest exes I've ever encountered was a man that I never had sex with or kissed (thankfully). Nevertheless, he felt like I was his property, and the day I met his controlling side was the day I ended my relationship with him. That guy would randomly show up at my job, call one of my family members or pass by my house, and he did this for two years after we broke up. And here's the amazing part—I wasn't afraid of him. I wasn't afraid of any of the narcissists I've dealt with. I was very confrontational and prideful; this is why I didn't get the cops involved. I was used to protecting myself. Over the course of my life, I'd become a wild animal and I'd lost all fear of people. I was either fearless or foolish; either way, I put myself in harm's way a LOT! And I mention that I was fearless because a lot of time when people think of women like myself—women who've dealt with a few crazies here and there, they often think of passive, fearful women. No! If you're prophetic in nature (which essentially is what an empath is), you will attract narcissists or, better yet, people who have the Jezebel spirit. These wild animals will romantically pursue you, financially pursue you, emotionally pursue you and spiritually pursue you. This is why you have to absolutely get in the will of God and stay there! And please note that Satan will always show you what you don't have. This is how he deceived Eve. He pointed out the one "no" in the garden of many "yeses." He'll point out that you're single; he'll point out that your friends who are in sin are accomplishing everything you've set out to accomplish. He'll point out everything that you don't have, and try to tempt you outside the will of God. He wants to, at minimum, get you back into the wilderness because if he can do this, he can bind you there, oftentimes by playing matchmaker.

The body is a sacrificial offering, believe it or not. You will submit it to one kingdom or the other; you will submit it to one god or the other. Of course, this is entirely dependent upon whatever imaginations and beliefs you're entertaining. If you have your heart and your eyes set on YAHWEH, you will present your body as a living sacrifice, holy and acceptable to Him, which is your reasonable service (see Romans 12:1). Howbeit, if there's an idol anywhere in your heart or in your sights, you will submit your body to that idol; that is, if you don't immediately pull it down. I can't tell you how many couples I've counseled who were on the verge of a divorce, and the mistake that they'd made was they'd built their marriages on the wrong foundations. This is going to sound inappropriate, but it's the truth. The problem was that somewhere in the cement of their foundation, there was semen, blood and a declaration (contract). And I'm not just talking about folks who "hooked up" while they were sinners, I'm talking about saved folks who love the Lord who'd dabbled in and traveled between both kingdoms in an attempt to get what they wanted! Kingdom people, like worldly people, tend to be impatient, and consequently, they are always trying to hijack their next seasons. These people had gone to counselors galore, but no one had been able to solve the complexity that was their marriage. You see, just like them, every other counselor saw weeds in the garden so they cut them down, dressed them up and hoped for the best, without dealing with the root of the issue. They didn't deal with the foundation! And surprisingly enough, the foundation wasn't sexual immorality; it wasn't the sexual sin that produced the problem! The sexual sin produced the ink for the contract (blood, semen and sweat). What then produced the problem? It was pure, unadulterated, unchecked idolatry; this is what led them into sexual immorality in the first place! And here's the thing about idolatry; it produces two types of people in a relationship. It produces the giver; this is the worshiper, the one who makes the majority of the sacrifices. This is the idolater; this is usually the most mature and most prophetic one in the duo. This is the one who's always trying to prove himself or herself to be loyal, loving and committed. Next, it produces the idol. This is typically the person who comes to enjoy being worshiped and reverenced. This is the person who is the least mature one in the relationship, but is the most entitled one. And please understand that this person didn't start off behaving in a malicious manner. It's just that over time, he or she got addicted to having his or her needs met first. Anything that comes first is an i-d-o-l! This essentially encouraged the worshiped one to become increasingly narcissistic and dependent on the worshiper. The worshiper, on the other hand, started feeling more and more drained, confused, desperate, frustrated and lost. The worshiped one or idol became increasingly demanding until the worshiper could no longer keep up with his or her demands. (Whatever you feed will grow, whatever you starve will die.) The worshiped one then started seeing himself or herself as a victim; consequently, his or her appetite for attention grew to the point where it began to consume the relationship. When the worshiper was unable to keep up with the demands of the narcissist, the worshiped one (idol, narcissist) went out and find someone else who was willing to worship him or her. Feeling justified and entitled, the worshiped one began to also despise the worshiper (empath, Ahab). Because the worshiper had made a lot of major sacrifices to be with the worshiped one, the worshiper had trouble letting go. Understand that some narcissists are born, while others are created. They are created by people who spoil and worship them; they are created by people who put them ahead of God. Any person who allows himself or herself to become an idol is a person who will begin to wrestle with the Jezebel spirit/narcissistic personality. Yes, you can meet someone who God has approved for your life—someone who loves and fears the Lord, and you can turn around and sabotage that relationship by (repeatedly) engaging in sexual misconduct with that person. This is because you are submitting your body as a sacrifice to that person and not to God. If the person accepts the offering, he or she will become a god in your life or vice versa.

Submit your body as a living sacrifice. *Living.* This means that it's going to hurt, it won't make sense and it will appear to have the opposite effect of what you want. You'll see seasoned and unseasoned believers in sexual immorality, and it will look like God is okay with or maybe even blessing their rebellion. No, it's just a mirage! What you're witnessing is idolatry, and if you ever have the privilege of sitting in on a counseling session of a couple who put their relationship ahead of God's Word, you will come to understand why God absolutely has to come first! After that encounter, you will likely become proactive in narcissist-proofing your life! I'm not saying that relationships like these cannot be redeemed, but in my experience, the relationship itself has to get saved. And what I mean by this is the old foundation has to be destroyed and a new one has to be built if that relationship is to survive! This sounds easy enough, but consider the dynamics. You have a worshiped one and a worshiper. The worshiper is oftentimes MORE THAN WILLING to repent, tear down the old foundation and build a relationship that gives God the glory. The worshiped one, on the other hand, is often unwilling to do this because doing so would require the worshiped one to humble himself or herself and give God back His seat in the other person's life. Honestly, it is easier to get Satan to admit he was wrong than it is to get a narcissist to repent. It's not impossible, just unlikely. And of course, there are those people who are holding onto hope that their narcissistic lovers will change their ways, and to this, they'd say, "I have faith! If God can make a donkey speak, He can change my husband!" I agree. The only thing

61

that God cannot do is tell a lie. Howbeit, God does not operate against the will of a human being. He allows us to choose right from wrong. So, whenever we pray for people, God does answer. He begins to soften their hearts (make them more empathetic), and He'll bring some people into their lives to show them the way. But it's important to note that He does not hijack their will; He simply gives them the space and the grace to repent. From there, they get to make a choice. Either they will serve the Lord and turn from their wicked ways, or they will serve the enemy and turn away from the Lord. This is why the Bible tells us that if the unbeliever wants to depart, let them depart.

You have to draw boundaries around your mind in order to draw boundaries around your body. I know that a lot of Christians dabble around in sexual immorality, but again, this is just the fruit of unbelief manifesting itself. Consequently, the divorce statistics are just as high in the church as they are in the world. If you want better results, don't date, court, marry or yoke yourself up with anyone you come across in the wilderness! This is because in order to keep that person, you will have to give a sin offering, and you will have to be willing to settle down in the jungle to keep that person. Sadly enough, most people who settle down in the wilderness eventually grow old and say, "I've never experienced what it's like to be loved by a man" or "I've never experienced what it's like to be loved by a woman." True, authentic, unconditional love is found in Christ. Your first assignment is to embrace His love, not just acknowledge it. As you do this, you will progress forward, slowly but surely, out of the wilderness and into your promised land. It is there that God will hide you so that your husband can find you, and if you're a guy, it is there that God will lead you to your wife. Don't allow impatience and idolatry to provoke you to drag something out of the woods, and then proceed to exchange vows with it. This is what the high priest did, but in reverse!

Leviticus 16:20-22 (ESV): And when he has made an end of atoning for the Holy Place and the tent of meeting and the altar, he shall present the live goat. And Aaron shall lay both his hands on the head of the live goat, and confess over it all the iniquities of the people of Israel, and all their transgressions, all their sins. And he shall put them on the head of the goat and send it away into the wilderness by the hand of a man who is in readiness. The goat shall bear all their iniquities on itself to a remote area, and he shall let the goat go free in the wilderness.

Relational Boundaries

I recently started watching Judge Judy, and like I've done with every other show I've liked, I've binge-watched it for some time now. I watched an episode recently where a woman was suing her sister. The Plaintiff (we'll call her Jessica) was suing her sister (we'll call her Camilla). Jessica appeared to be between 32-35 years old. She was beautiful and appeared to be what some would call "cultured." I was shocked when she said that she was over 50 years old. It was obvious to me that she'd enjoyed the finer things in life because of how she carried herself. Camilla, on the other hand, looked to be between 48-55 years old, and she looked every bit of her age, but for whatever reason, I could tell that Jessica was older than Camilla, even though she looked younger.

Judge Judy started with the Plaintiff. "Okay, tell me what happened" she said, turning her seat towards Jessica. The moment Jessica began speaking, I had pretty much already summarized the case in my mind. It was clear to me that Camilla envied her sister, but I had to keep watching to confirm or nullify my suspicions. Please note that this had nothing to do with their appearances; it had everything to do with their postures. Jessica faced the judge with confidence. It was clear to me that she hadn't expected the turn of events that had taken place between her and her sister. Camilla's posture revealed her hatred and envy towards her sister. She slightly angled her body away from her sister and could barely look in her direction. All the same, she kept looking at the table (which is a sign of guilt). As it turned out, Jessica had fallen on hard times (I think she'd gone through a divorce). And because of this, she'd asked her sister, Camilla, if she could come and live with her and her family until she got back on her feet. Camilla agreed. Jessica moved in with Camilla, and less than a week later, they'd had what should have been a small disagreement. I don't remember what they'd fought about, but what I do remember is that they'd had a small difference of opinion, and Camilla used that as an opportunity to berate and physically assault her sister. In short, she overreacted. She even demanded that her sister leave her home immediately. I growled at the television set because I absolutely abhor jealousy, envy, competition and comparison. Nevertheless, I kept watching because I wanted to see how the case ended. All the same, I'd just heard one side of the story. Maybe, when it was Camilla's turn to speak, I'd realize that I was wrong and it would turn out that Jessica had been the problematic one. That didn't happen. Camilla finally got her chance, and the minute she began to speak, she confirmed everything that I thought. She used language like:

- "She thinks she's better than everybody!"
- "She's so uppity that ..."
- "If she'd come down to Earth, she'd realize ..."

She didn't use those phrases exactly, but she'd said

something to that effect. When she'd lifted her head, Camilla smiled mischievously like she was proud of how she'd handled her sister. She looked at the judge and she could barely defend her actions. Her sister had led a better life than her, and for that, she needed to be punished; that is, at least, in Camilla's eyes. In Camilla's opinion, her sister needed to be humbled. Some people would ask, "Why would she allow Jessica to come and live with her if she was jealous of her?" The answer is simple—it's culture! I have family members who would happily open up their homes for me if I fell on hard times, but they despise me with every fiber of their being. They'd do it because:

1. We're family (It's American culture).
2. Just to hear about my fall from glory.
3. So they could tell me how they really feel about me.
4. To charge me an arm and a leg in rent.

Within a week or two, they'd throw me out of their homes for something as small as me parting my hair on the left when they told me that it looked better on the right. People like Camilla have to be kept at arm's length because they are not only toxic, they are dangerous! Judge Judy ended up throwing the case out because what Jessica referred to as an assault was nothing more than her sister shoving her and getting in her face. Camilla's counter-claim was dismissed as well because she was suing her sister for false arrest, even though she'd already plead guilty to assaulting her sister in another court case (I don't remember the actual charge). After the case was dismissed, as always, the camera crew interviewed both the Plaintiff and the Defendant outside the courtroom, and Camilla's jealousy could barely contain itself. (Spirits will stop at nothing to express themselves.) You see, jealous people have certain labels or phrases they use to categorize the people that they're jealous of. These labels include:

- "You think you're better than everybody!"
- "Somebody needs to knock you off your high horse!"
- "What goes up must come down!"
- "You need to get your head out of the clouds!"
- "You bleed red just like everybody else!"

Now, this isn't to say that EVERYONE who uses these phrases are manifesting jealousy towards another human being, but this is to say that these phrases are commonplace for people who wrestle with competition and comparison. When someone is jealous of you, that person will develop a thought-process about you that's not only unrealistic, but most of what that person believes about you will be untrue. And no amount of reasoning will help them to see what God has blinded them to; that is, your potential! In Jessica's case, I'm pretty sure that she knew her sister didn't have a good heart towards her, howbeit, like most people, she likely hoped that she'd either had a change of heart regarding her or she hoped she could change her sister's mind. Nevertheless, the Bible tells us that jealousy is as cruel as the grave, and believe me when I say that these words couldn't be any truer. The most dangerous person you could have in your intimate space is a person who envies you! This is because such a soul will have little to no grace, no love and no mercy towards you. This is why Camilla overreacted. She wasn't just responding to the slight offense, she was responding to all of the pint-up hatred that she had towards her sister. Standing outside of the courtroom, she talked about how her sister had always had money, and pretty much everything unrelated to the case. Her fascination with and hatred towards her sister had everything to do with her sister's life and lifestyle, not her character.

It is absolutely imperative that you draw relational boundaries around yourself to keep these types of people at a safe distance! Most people don't realize that their inability to move forward in life is directly connected to who they've surrounded themselves with and who they've decided to tolerate. Yes, this includes parents! Please understand that you don't necessarily have to cut every toxic person out of your life. Oftentimes, you simply need to reposition them. This is because every level of access to your heart should have a certain measure of security. Remember, God told us to guard our hearts. Why? Because out it flows the issues of life! Howbeit, we live in a day and age where people absolutely demand a trust that they have not earned, and sadly enough, their narcissistic ramblings are oftentimes enough to get some people to lower their guards at the expense of their sanity and their sanctity. What you'll come to learn is, every person in your life can only handle a certain measure of you and a certain side of you. Listen, you're multifaceted; this means that there are many dimensions of you and many sides to you. This is why you are cool, collected, calm and reserved around some people, but when you're around others, you are loud, silly, energetic and outgoing. You're not being fake; you're simply giving each person the side of you that they're pulling on! It's like spinning you around to find the face that they prefer to see. And when you're around new people or new faces, you may be extremely quiet and appear to be shy, but as they get to know you, they'll soon discover that you are far from timid. You joked a little, preached a little and maybe even shared a story. You were looking to see which side of your character they were going to respond to. This is human nature! You may even discover that you've never considered introducing one friend of yours to another, even though you've introduced them both to another set of friends. This is generally because one or both of those particular friends have never seen the other side of you, and you don't think they can handle it. Your friend who's only seen you praying, reading the Bible and cracking a few church jokes may not know how to handle the silly, non-religious side of you, and that's okay! She'll pull on the side of you that brings out the best (or the worst) in her.

Additionally, I've seen many cases on Judge Judy where relationships have been destroyed because of money. Most of us have heard our parents or our grandparents say, "Don't loan out any money that you can't afford to give away." In other words, there is a possibility that the person won't pay you back, and if this would make it difficult or impossible for you to pay a bill, eat or commute to work, don't loan the money out. This wisdom has often fallen on deaf ears because we've been pulled in by our heartstrings to one of our friends or family member's sob stories. And then the time came for them to pay us back, and we silently hoped that they'd do so without us having to ask for the money or remind them that they owed us money. But this rarely happens. Instead, most people who have money management issues will simply avoid you when they have the money to pay you back. Understand this—a person will only be as good to you as they are to their bill collectors.

I saw another case on Judge Judy recently where a man was suing his former best friend because she'd borrowed a thousand dollars from him, and she'd failed to return it. Cases like these are common. What generally happens is, one friend will constantly loan money to the other friend, and the borrower always follows through with repaying the money. That is, until the lender loaned the borrower a certain amount of money. Here's what you need to know—in the large majority of relationships that you are a part of, you have a certain measure of value to each person who are you involved with. Going back to the Judge Judy case, the guy had loaned his best friend a thousand dollars, and she'd decided not to return it. This means that their friendship was not worth a thousand dollars to her, but get this—she'd borrowed money from him many times in the past, and she'd always been diligent about returning it. Nevertheless, this was the first time he'd loaned her a thousand bucks. What this tells us is that whenever he'd loaned her a hundred dollars, she'd decided that one hundred dollars was not worth her losing his friendship. Whenever he'd loaned her five hundred dollars, she'd decided that five hundred dollars was not worth her losing his friendship. However, when he'd loaned her a thousand dollars, she'd decided that he wasn't worth her losing a thousand bucks. I call this an expensive lesson and an expensive deliverance. You may have some friends who wouldn't trade you for a million dollars, but they'd shove you into alligator-infested waters for two million bucks and a slice of pizza. But you may be safe with them for the rest of your life if you never become a millionaire. Then again, there may be some people in your life who value a five-dollar bill more than they value their relationship with you. If they saw five dollars sticking out your pocket, they'd steal it. If they saw five dollars on the floor of your car, they'd steal it. If you confronted them, they'd berate, belittle and maybe even assault you.

What's the point of all this? In summary, the key to success, peace and happiness is the proper placement or arrangement of people in your life. This requires you first taking inventory of your relationships so that you can differentiate between associates, mentees, friends, close friends and best friends. A lot of the anxiety and warfare we deal with on a daily basis is largely due to the misplacement of people in our lives. With each category, there has to be a certain measure of access. For example, I can be wholly open and transparent with someone I call my best friend. I can share some intimate details of my life with close friends. With a friend, my conversations would not be as intimate; they'd mainly be surface-level, meaning, we'd talk about what's evident and maybe somethings that I don't consider to be too personal. With an associate, I'd talk about sports, traveling and life in general. I would not discuss anything personal, including my political views with an associate. This is because you can give a person more information that he or she can handle, and this will almost always be detrimental to the relationship you have with that person. Not everyone can have intimate access to you. Consider the case of Jessica and Camilla. While they are both sisters, it is clear that Camilla's heart towards Jessica is dark, and get this—no amount of therapy can fix this. And while I HIGHLY suggest therapy for most issues that arise in relationships, I would advise you against bringing or keeping envious people close to you because jealousy is unreasonable. In other words, you can't reason with or domesticate a demon! I know that it's difficult having to love some people from afar, especially when they're parents or siblings of yours, but you should always prioritize your mental health and your quality of life over toxic relationships. And sometimes, you have to give people the ability to hurt or disappoint you on a smaller scale just so you can see where they should be in your life. For example, when I was younger, I worked at Walmart, and while working there, I'd somewhat befriended a woman who we'll call Penny. She wasn't a friend of mine per se, but she hung around me and my friends, plus, we'd went to lunch together a few times. All the same, Penny was trying to get closer to me, even though she was significantly older than me. She'd invited me to travel out of the state with her a few times, and she would always say that we needed to hang out more. I had traveled out of state with her once, and it was on that trip that I decided that Penny and I simply could not be friends because she was way too argumentative.

One day, Penny asked me where I was going for lunch. It was a Thursday, so I knew where she wanted to go. There was a restaurant just across the street from our workplace that everybody in town seemed to frequent on Thursdays. This is because they had the best chicken dressing around, and they only served it on Thursdays. I happily agreed to go to lunch with Penny, so we both headed to the back to clock out and get out purses out of our lockers. I remember that I had $27 to my name. The dressing plate always cost seven dollars even, so I was going to have a little less than $20 left (I always left a tip). Once we got our purses, I told Penny that I needed to stop at the bathroom right quick. "Okay," she said. "I'll hold your purse so you don't have to put it on that dirty floor." At first, I resisted. "No, I'll hang it on the door," I said. But Penny was insistent. She held out her hand in a motherly fashion, and being as it was that she was double my age, I went ahead and complied. But I knew deep down within that I was going to regret handing her my purse. Howbeit, I decided to take a chance because, I reasoned, if she was the snake I believed her to be, she'd prove it to me that day. I handed Penny my purse and rushed on into the bathroom. I was probably in there for less than two minutes, but when I finally emerged from the bathroom, Penny was nowhere to be found. However, she'd placed my purse on one of the tables in the lounge and left it there unattended. I remember feeling dread and gloom in that moment. I knew that she'd stolen my money, but something in me wanted to be wrong. "Penny!" I shouted her name several times. After a minute or two, she came back into the lounge. "Why did you leave my purse unattended?!" I asked. Penny looked absolutely guilty and afraid. "Oh, I just stepped out real quick. I figured no one was going to mess with it." As Penny spoke, I reached out and grabbed my purse, and when she saw that I was opening it, she tried to stop me. "Nobody's been in your purse! Let's go so we can beat the lunch rush!" I didn't listen. I angrily began to unzip my purse, and that's when Penny tried to snatch it, but of course, she wasn't successful. "Come on, let's go!" she said with her voice quivering. "You know how packed Gus can get." I completely ignored her, pulled out my wallet and opened it up. Seven dollars. That's all I had left to my name. She'd stolen my twenty-dollar bill and left me seven dollars, which again was the exact amount of a plate lunch from Gus's Restaurant. And while I was livid, I also felt a sense of gratitude. Penny could no longer come anywhere near me, and I made sure of that. A month or two later, she was arrested after being caught stealing on the job. You see, there are times when you have to risk something small to get rid of someone who may prove to be a big problem in your life. Getting rid of Penny cost me twenty dollars, but it was money well-spent. The same is true for relatives. Sometimes, loaning a relative a small amount of money is enough for them to show you their character so that you can reposition that relative in (or outside) of your life. When you test the spirits in people (which is what the Bible tells us to do), and you position them accordingly, you unclog God's blessings in your life. Consider the story of Abram. He could only go so far with Lot trailing him, and it wasn't until he sent Lot away that he finally heard from God again (see Genesis 13). Abram had to set relational boundaries around himself in order for him to hear from God. The same is true for us. I've had countless growth spurts and sudden breakthroughs by simply doing what Abram did; that is, putting space and distance between myself and some of the people I had in my life. And like Abram, I didn't have to cut them all the way off; I just had to go my way and let them go their way, and whenever they found themselves in a spiritual fight, I was there to pray with them and for them. In other words, I wasn't mad at them; I didn't have any ill-will towards them in my heart. I'd just decided that they were too toxic or entitled to be as close to me as they were. I literally have people in my life who only call me for prayer, and I'm okay with that. Why? Because I've placed the right labels on those relationships. Offense is the product of a misplaced label. If I realize that someone I called a friend is a mentee and not a friend, I'm okay with it as long as we both acknowledge and understand our roles with one another. Some people, for example, love the friend tag, but whenever you open yourself up for a friendship with them, they will take way more than they give. They'll spend the next few years saying, "Thank you," and at some point, you're going to get tired of feeling used and saying, "You're welcome." You're going to want to have something to come out of that relationship that you can be thankful for as well, and not just a bunch of well-placed compliments! But if you realize that the person is a mentee and you are that person's mentor, you won't avail yourself to be used so frequently. You see, in mentor/mentee relationships, the mentor's goal is to mature and equip the mentee to stand on his or her own two feet. In a mentor/mentee relationship, the mentor does most of the pouring (impartation). But the mentee has to balance the relationship by being a blessing as well. For example, let's imagine that you are a fashion designer, and not just that, but you've done fairly well in the world of fashion. You haven't gotten the notoriety that you deserve just yet, but you have managed to make a name for yourself.

One day, a woman walks up to you and says, "I've been to all of your shows, and I've literally bought all of your books! I absolutely admire your work. I am an up-and-coming fashion designer as well, and I've been praying for a mentor. I would love if you would be willing to mentor me." What this person is literally asking for is your time and your resources. People literally pay for this! First and foremost, such a request can be relatively offensive to most designers, nevertheless, you like the young woman's style and her boldness, so after seeing her portfolio, you agree to mentor her. One day, she calls you and says, "I really want to pick your brain. What are you doing Friday night?" You tell her about a show you're hosting, but the show should be over by nine that evening, so you agree to go out to dinner with her. On Friday, you show up at the restaurant and the two of you order your food. While waiting on the food, she asks you a lot of questions, all of which you answer. Two hours later, the two of you wipe your mouths and ask the waiter for the ticket. "Will this be one or two tickets?" he asks. The mentee abruptly answers. "Two, please." Immediately, you feel offense rising up. Do you have the right to be offended? Absolutely! This was not a date between two friends where there was an equal pour. You were literally working for free, so the least she could have done was picked up the tab. Now, this may not be offensive the first time, but if she makes a habit of this, it could become a problem. Nevertheless, we live in a time where entitlement has become normalized and some people find the notion of a two-sided relationship offensive. Consequently, the poor get poorer and the rich get richer. This isn't just a capitalism issue; the issue is entitlement. A person who refuses to invest in their own development is a liability in every sense of the word, and most builders know this! How so? Most builders have invested in people who did nothing but take, take and take, only stopping to give a few compliments and "thank you's" here and there. People like this quit way too easily because they don't have an equal share or investment into the relationship. This is why professionals have to establish boundaries, and one of the most effective boundaries that an entrepreneur can set is called an invoice. Invoices separate the entitled (those full of pride) from the hungry. What I always recommend for entrepreneurs is that they:

1. Create a website and list all of their services and prices. For example, let's revisit the woman who walked up to a fashion designer and asked to be mentored. If that fashion designer has a website where she lists her mentoring fees, she could avoid having a bunch of long, drawn out conversations with people who think everyone is supposed to invest in them, even though they refuse to invest in themselves. She could say, "Sure, I'd love to! Here's my business card. You'll find information about my mentorship program on my site." If she doesn't have a website, she may find herself having to tell the woman about her fees, and then, being inundated with questions and long, extremely detailed sob stories. Every entrepreneur has experienced this, and it is for this reason that serious professionals establish websites or, at minimum, landing pages.

2. Get business cards. This establishes to the person you're speaking with that you have an official business. When people think your business is nothing more than a glorified hobby, they'll waste a lot of your time asking for favors and advice. In truth, I don't think most business owners and professionals mind giving out advice here and there, however, it can become extremely time-consuming at some point. Having business cards allows you to point people to your website, where they can find answers to their questions.

3. Never allow someone to share a long personal story when they are addressing you professionally. In my experience, people can talk nonstop for hours on end when they simply don't want to pay you.

These are just a few tips that I give. The point is, you have to draw boundaries around yourself relationally, otherwise, you will find yourself constantly being taken advantage of. And believe me when I say that there are many people on the face of this planet who have been traumatized by takers, especially people who have the gift of charity. The newer translations of the Bible refer to this as the gift of love, and while this is true, it does not describe this dimension of love. The gift of charity, simply put, is a love that compels you to give. People who have this gift feel invigorated, energized and excited every time they serve as a blessing to another person. The problem with this is that a large number of people are takers, and takers can and do traumatize givers. This is because after repeatedly giving to people and getting nothing but a "thank you" in return, it's natural to feel taken advantage of. This feeling eventually graduates to guilt and then to you feeling "stupid," meaning, you begin to channel your anger towards yourself. This horrible feeling can be very intense for empathetic (prophetic) people so much so that if you experience it, you may reason within yourself that you'll never give to someone again. The problem is you're wired to give, so when this gift is stopped up or clogged up, it creates another issue: anxiety. Again, you have to draw boundaries around yourself relationally, and you do this by putting the proper labels on every relationship. And it doesn't just end there. Every label should have allowances, for example, if someone who is serving as a mentor in my life was to call me, that person's calls would have precedence over every other call; this is because that person is pouring into me. All the same, I would balance our relationship by finding a way to give back to the mentor, rather than just taking his or her time and not giving anything in return. This is called honor. Again, you should always find ways to balance out your relationships. Now granted, with friends, there will be seasons where your friends will be pouring into you and seasons where you'll be pouring into them, but in mentee/mentorship relationships, the mentor does all the pouring all the time. This is why you should find a way to balance it out. If not, the mentorship will grow into a one-sided friendship and the mentor will start feeling used and unappreciated.

In summary, we all have a Camilla somewhere lurking, and we have all had our fair share of users. But the goal wasn't to get mad at them. The lesson is called REPOSITIONING. When you assign the proper roles to everyone in your life (according to where they are on the spectrum of maturity), you will have peace on every side. Sometimes, frustration, anxiety, depression and anger come from you not listening to that quiet, still voice within that says, "She's not your friend" or "He's not the one for you." Consequently, you may find yourself serving time with folks that you were only supposed to encourage, edify and love from afar. This isn't because they are undeserving of your time, it's because they don't have enough love, understanding or grace to be as close to you as they want to be. One of the most profound lessons I've learned is that if I want to increase the lifespan of my relationships, it is imperative that I not allow people, for example, to call me their "best friend" when they don't have the capacity to be a friend. You see, the word "best friend" comes with a great amount of expectation and responsibility, and this is why so many people throw this label around so freely, especially when they're in their twenties and early thirties. Get this—it is possible for you to be someone's best friend, while that person is but a friend to you. What this means is, you give in and of yourself in that relationship. That person can fully and wholeheartedly rely on you to be there for him or her in hard times and in good times. Let's say that this is a female friend of yours. She knows that she can call you anytime of the day, and you will stop whatever it is that you're doing and avail yourself to her. But you don't have that luxury in return. You're not a top priority in her life, even though she will tell the whole wide world that you're her best friend. (I've been in this situation more times than I care to recount). As a matter of fact, your friend sends you to voicemail more times than you care to count, but she expects you to answer all of her calls or, at minimum, to return them expeditiously. She compliments you. She says she's so grateful for your friendship, and while her words are laced with honey, her actions are as sour as lemon peels. Most of us have spent years upon years with people like this, constantly giving our time and our resources to them, only for them to give us a bunch of "thank you's" and public praise reports in return. Don't get me wrong—I'm not saying that people like this should be avoided at all costs. What I am saying is that you have to put the right labels on these relationships or you'll find yourself constantly wanting to rid your life of those people and not knowing why you feel the way you feel. Get this—the desire to get rid of them is your heart's alarm going off, saying that they are too close and consequently, are doing some damage to your heart. In truth, friends like these made me not want to have "best friends" or friends that got too close. I had to heal from this and realize that I'd allowed a bunch of immature people in my life, and honestly, I let them tell me who I was to them, and I assumed that I was supposed to say the same in return. It was and is not uncommon for me to hear someone say, "You're my best friend. I know we haven't known each other long, but I feel like I can tell you anything." From there, they would publicly affirm me as their best friend and I felt the need to say the same in return. Months or years later, I'd find myself frustrated every time I found myself needing someone to talk to, and not being able to get that from them. I remember confronting a former friend of mine about this. I said to her, "Over the five years that I've known you, you have never been there for me. I've literally held the phone and cried about things I was going through, all the while, listening to you talk nonstop about yourself and about some of the most minute issues. I've had to comfort you while I was broken." I brought to her attention one incident where I'd just gotten what was packaged as a prophetic word about

God preparing to take my mother, and I was extremely heartbroken. My mother had just come out of surgery and she wasn't looking so good. I'd cried nonstop the entire day, and when I spoke to this particular friend, she simply said, "I know it's hard when the people we love leave us, but just know that God will comfort you." After that, as usual, she shifted the conversation back to herself and she talked nonstop about her workplace offenses. I hadn't realized that this had become a norm in our friendship until that moment. When I brought this to her attention, she surprised me with these words, "Oh wow. I just thought you were strong enough to handle your problems on your own. My apologies for thinking you were stronger than you actually are." Yes, she actually said that! And of course, I confronted her, but after this, I started putting boundaries in place. I decided that I didn't want to keep being her best friend/mentor while she served as an acquaintance in my life. People love placing the wrong labels on relationships so they can get the most out of those relationships. If you give people their rightful places in your life, you will have peace with them, but because they want the benefits that come with mislabeling the relationship, they will absolutely insist, for example, that they are your best friends when, in truth, they may be friends, acquaintances or mentees. Now, this doesn't make them bad people; in most cases, it simply means that they are immature. To remedy this, you simply have to see if they are mature enough to fill the roles that they want to assume, and if not, be okay with telling them where they fit. Explain to them that friendships are a two-way street, and then require that they give as much as they take. This is normally enough to chase away most narcissists.

Ask the Holy Spirit to help you place everyone in your life in their rightful places. And be sure to have allowances and boundaries associated with each label. Don't allow people to repeatedly cross those boundaries, after all, offense is the product of a crossed boundary. If someone crosses a boundary, just remind that person of the boundary. For example, if someone I'm mentoring calls me at twelve in the morning, obviously, I'm going to answer the phone to make sure everything is okay. But if that person just wants to ask a bunch of questions, "shoot the breeze" or complain about life, I will let that person know that they are out of bounds. In other words, I may say, "In the future, don't call me so late. This wasn't that big of a deal. Try texting me no later than 10pm and no earlier than 10am in the future. Late night calls make me think that something is wrong." What I'm doing is protecting my relationship with that person by not allowing her to passively transition the mentorship into a friendship when she doesn't yet know how to be a friend. Everything that's healthy and sound is guarded by rules. Anything that has little to no rules is an open door for the enemy. You can build some solid, lifelong and healthy relationships with people if you establish and enforce rules. And lastly, please note that this doesn't mean that they shouldn't have rules in regards to you. They should have them, after all, this is a two-way street! But there has to be a mutual understanding as to your roles with one another; this is how you keep confusion and offense out of the relationship, and this is how the both of you get the maximum benefits out of whatever it is that you are building. And remember, don't loan out anymore money than you can afford to give away. Every person has a certain measure of value that they've attached to your name, and whenever God takes you out of that particular realm of thought (season), He will cause the people who value your resources more than they value their relationship with you to fall away. Sometimes, He will use you to finance their exit from your life. Just keep going and keep growing, and remember—everything you build needs boundaries. This includes relationships—platonic, romantic, professional and familial!

VERBAL BOUNDARIES

James 1:26: If any man among you seem to be religious, and bridleth not his tongue, but deceiveth his own heart, this man's religion is vain.

James 3:2: For in many things we offend all. If any man offend not in word, the same is a perfect man, and able also to bridle the whole body.

Matthew 15:11: Not that which goeth into the mouth defileth a man; but that which cometh out of the mouth, this defileth a man.

In the previous section, we talked a lot about relationships, along with the power and purpose of physical boundaries. In this section, we're going to look at the power of words and come to understand why what we say is important. First off, your words create your world. Look around you right now. Everything that you see is a product of your belief system and your confessions. Log into your bank account right now. Your balance is a reflection of your faith, your declarations and your decisions. Your reality is the picture that's produced by your choices—and by choices, I don't mean your words and your works. Again, we've established that your works are nothing but fruits. Consider this—if you were a tree in my garden, and I was a farmer, my job would be to water and to cultivate you; my job would be to grow you up so that you can produce fruit and eventually begin to reproduce after yourself. In other words, you'd grow to not only produce fruit, but to produce other trees like yourself. This is what increases the size of my garden, and ultimately, the size of your harvest. Howbeit, if I discovered one day that the fruits you're producing are contaminated with fornication, anger and pride, it wouldn't benefit either of us if I simply picked all the fruits from your branches and tossed them into a landfill. Why? Because you would continue to produce that same fruit until I dealt with the soil. This is the grounds or foundation that you're rooted in. This is the core of your belief system. In other words, there's something in the soil that's getting into your roots and ultimately affecting your harvest. So, to remedy this, I may have to uproot you and either move you or look at the soil composition. According to GreenTumble.com, in order to repair damaged soil, I'd have to:

1. Drain the land
2. Replenish its nutrients
3. Alkalize it
4. Prepare the mulch
5. Bioremediation

(Source: GreenTumble.com/Repairing Damaged Soil for Sustainable Farming/Emily Folk)

Draining the Land

This means that the soil has to be excavated in some areas so that the farmer can see what's possibly affecting or infecting it. In most cases, the farmer will find water under the soil that's potentially coming from a contaminated source. The farmer then has to place drain pipes in the ground to drain that water and any more water that will come from that source.

Replenish its Nutrients

During the draining process, the ground will lose a lot of nutrients, and these nutrients are a necessity for the plants in that ground to survive. So, the farmer has to replenish or restore the soil by infusing it with the minerals it will need to be revived.

Alkalize It

The pH balance of the soil has to be restored to neutrality, so farmers will typically add wood ashes, oyster shells and soil to neutralize the soil.

Prepare the Mulch

Soil alone can once again lose its nutrients, and its pH balance can be brought low if the soil isn't covered or protected. Mulch, dry leaves and straw help to protect and preserve the soil's additives, thus, increasing the likelihood of healthy plant growth.

Bioremediation

In this, farmers use live organisms to remove the contaminants that are present in the soil.

So, if I was a farmer and you were a tree producing bad fruits, I'd have to look at the grounds you're planted in to see where you are getting your information from. I'd also have to look at your roots because the roots of a tree can stretch out up to twenty feet in length and in depth! That's nearly a mile! In other words, I'd have to trace your words and your choices all the way down to their roots until I found what (or who) you are sourcing from. Next, I'd have to drain it or, better yet, flood you with truth until you stop sourcing from the lie. This can take weeks, months and years, depending on how teachable you are! Then, I'd have to replenish the nutrients; this has to deal with the voids in your soul. I'd have to fill those voids with revelation; that is, the Word of God so that the empty spaces can be made whole and illuminated. Next, I'd have to teach you the importance of honor and community; this way, you won't get offended and uproot yourself. And finally, for your remediation, I'd have to deal with the residue. This is done through counseling and deliverance. Sounds like a great pastor, right? What if I told you that this is your job! You are both the farmer and the tree; you are responsible for examining yourself and submitting yourself to another person to be examined, corrected, pruned and grown. For example, one of the world's beliefs that has somehow crept into the church is the belief that good sex is powerful enough to make another human being fall in love. How did this creep in? It's simple. A lot of believers have not removed themselves from the world; they have not sanctified themselves, therefore, they are physically in the church, but their beliefs are rooted in the world. The fact of the matter is, sex (within itself) only serves to "secure" an agreement between two people. As I mentioned earlier, it is the ink on the contract. For example, consider the story I shared about the crazed ex. Yes, we were engaging in premarital sex, but it wasn't the sex that made him behave the way that he did. The problem was that he had not guarded his heart. When we'd started dating, he'd allowed his imaginations to take over. Understand that the imagination is directly attached to the mind, will and emotions (soul). This is why God told us to cast down imaginations and every high thing that exalts itself against the knowledge of God and bring into captivity every thought to the obedience of Christ. He wasn't saved, so he didn't know this. He believed, without seeing any fruits of mine, that I was the woman he'd someday marry and have children with. He believed that a broken, half-dressed and prideful woman had the potential to become everything that he needed to fill his voids. Sure, I think it's obvious today that I definitely had potential, but no human being had the reach or the wherewithal to pull that potential out of me. I had to submit myself to God, and when (and only when) that happened, a human being could then begin to pull on my potential, but not necessarily pull it out. That's what the Word does! So, he started making confessions and ensnaring his soul way too soon. Being a love-starved creature, I adored hearing a man talking about marrying me, having children with me, providing for me, protecting me and just being a great husband. But as broken and as love-starved as I was, I also had enough B.C. (before Christ) discernment (we call this common sense) to know that the man I was dating was not the man I'd someday marry. After I'd seen his jealous side a couple of times, I knew that we wouldn't work out. But like most broken women, I stuck around because I adored being held, touched, affirmed and even worshiped. So, I matched his words with my own. I talked about marrying him, having children with him and I promised to stick by his side through thick and thin. In other words, we exchanged vows. We exchanged vows over the phone, we exchanged vows over dinner and we exchanged vows in the bedroom. In other words, we both ensnared our souls. This is what provoked him to behave the way that he did! This is the power of words! The point is, sex is only as powerful as the agreement you've made with the person you're having sex with OR your beliefs about that person. In other words, sex is eighty to ninety percent mental and contractual, and only ten to twenty percent physical. For example, have you ever heard someone say that "ugly men have the best sex?" If you've been in the world, chances are, you've heard this lie. The women who believed and promoted this foolishness would repeatedly have heightened sexual encounters with men who society deemed to be unattractive, not because the men were skilled; this had everything to do with their belief system! Because they believed this, every time they slept with someone who was visually unappealing, they expected to have a heightened experience with that person, therefore, they did. When they started confessing and promoting this lie, it only intensified their beliefs and their encounters. Again, sex is eighty to ninety percent mental and contractual;

how you respond to what happens in the bedroom is mainly reliant on your belief system. This is why a married woman can refuse to have sex with her husband for weeks or, in some cases, months on end. The problem is that mentally, she's not satisfied with her husband, and this dissatisfaction manifests itself in the bedroom because of how she feels about him as a person.

The Bible tells us to bridle our tongues. A bridle is a form of headgear placed on horses to govern their movements. In other words, what God was instructing/warning us to do was to exercise self-control over our mouths. This doesn't just mean that we are to refrain from saying things that may be hurtful or rude, but it also means to know when to speak and when to be silent. This is the epitome of self-control. Ecclesiastes 3:1-8 confirms this. It reads, "For everything there is a season, and a time for every matter under heaven: a time to be born, and a time to die; a time to plant, and a time to pluck up what is planted; a time to kill, and a time to heal; a time to break down, and a time to build up; a time to weep, and a time to laugh;
a time to mourn, and a time to dance; a time to cast away stones, and a time to gather stones together; a time to embrace, and a time to refrain from embracing; a time to seek, and a time to lose; a time to keep, and a time to cast away; a time to tear, and a time to sew; a time to keep silence, and a time to speak; a time to love, and a time to hate; a time for war, and a time for peace." If only the body of Christ would only meditate on this scripture! Much of what

we call warfare these days is nothing but the product of an unbridled tongue! Proverbs 21:23 proves this; it reads, "Those who guard their mouths and their tongues keep themselves from calamity."

When you were in elementary school, did you ever try to create a model volcano? If you did, you more than likely mixed baking soda with vinegar to simulate the lava that flowed from your makeshift volcano. Sciencing reports:
> "Baking soda has the chemical name sodium bicarbonate. Vinegar is a combination of water and 5 percent acetic acid. Since both materials contain chemicals, when the two combine there is a chemical reaction. When vinegar and baking soda are mixed, a new chemical called carbonic acid is made. This carbonic acid immediately decomposes into carbon dioxide gas. When you mix the vinegar and baking soda, it's the carbon dioxide gas that makes the bubbles."
> (Source: Sciencing.com/What Happens When You Mix Baking Soda With Vinegar to Inflate a Balloon?)

If you've ever tried this experiment, you stood by and watched the liquid boil, rise and then begin to overflow around the sides of your model volcano. You soon learned that some chemicals don't mix well together; whenever they are exposed to one another, they produce a reaction. The same concept should be applied to relationships. There are some people who may not pair well with you. For example, have you ever had a family member or a friend who loved to take advantage of people? You knew this about that person, after all, he or she had a reputation for always being in need. So, you vowed within your heart to never give anything to that individual. Nevertheless, one day, you received a call from that person (let's say she's your cousin), and she announced that she was on her way over to your house. After hanging up the phone, you vowed within your heart that you wouldn't give her any money, you wouldn't let her take up too much of your time and you wouldn't share any intimate details with her about your life. Five hours later, the two of you bid each other farewell. She stuffed the twenty dollar bill in her pocket and picked up three plates covered with aluminum foil while trying to carry three other bags. "I'll get them!" you said. "You have too much in your hands already." She let out a muzzled "thank you" because she was still chewing on her last bite of cake. The two of you walked outside and were greeted by the cool night air. She finally gulped the cake down, opened up her car door and started loading everything in. "Go back in the house and get those two bags of shoes!" you yelled at your oldest son. "They're in my bedroom, right next to my nightstand!" You then turned back around and hugged your cousin. "Thank you so much," she said. "You are like a big sister to me! You're always blessing me! And like I said, you know our kinfolks are crazy. Don't let them get to you. They're just jealous of your success." A few minutes later, your son emerged with the two bags, and after fifteen more minutes of small-talk, you went ahead and bid your relative farewell. As soon as she pulled out of the driveway, guilt bore down on you like a pile of rocks. You felt used, taken advantage of and downright stupid! "Why does this always happen?" you ask yourself. The simple answer is this—you're wired to give; she's wired to take. It's a simple chemical reaction that takes place whenever the two of you come together. But of course, it's a little more complex than that. You have what the older translations of the Bible refer to as the "gift of charity." Again, this is a dimension of love that compels you to give in and of yourself. Most empaths (prophetic people) have the gift of charity; we have a supernatural ability to love people beyond their faults. This is how we're wired, and we sometimes hate it! We are energized, encouraged and even revived whenever we bless somebody, however, this part of our makeup can be and oftentimes is hijacked by the narcissistic personality. A narcissist knows the password to the empath's heart; it's a four letter word. No, it's not love, it's time! You see, most prophetic people (empaths) are introverted, and introverts tend to lose virtue (energy, strength) whenever they are in the presence of other people. So, when your cousin came over, chances are, you were able to guard your heart for about an hour or two. After that, you lowered your guard and started sharing a few intimate details about your life. Your cousin looked at you with compassion in her big, puppy dog eyes, and for whatever reason, she started looking innocent and harmless to you. Slowly, but surely, you found yourself opening your mouth more, and before long, you'd thrown all of your inhibitions to the wind. And after your heart was hijacked, you felt that oh-so-familiar gift of charity creeping up on you. You tried to resist it, but it was too strong. "What size do you wear?" The question was completely unrelated to what the two of you were discussing, but love just gripped your heart as your cousin sat there and talked about her life and the changes she's trying to make in her life. An hour later, she walked out of your house with a new wardrobe and enough food to feed herself for two days! She also walked out of there knowing way too much about you! This is why it's important to know how you're wired; if not, the narcissistic personality will continue to wear down your defenses, get you to open your heart and your mouth, and then, get you to open your wallet! There are some people you simply do not mix well with because they can get you to cross verbal boundaries that you don't normally cross! And every time you leave their presence, you'll feel dirty, grimy, guilty and stupid! This means that in order for you to draw a boundary around your lips, you have to draw a boundary around your time and your presence. For example, I'm prophetic, meaning, I'm empathetic. I will only spend two hours or more around people who are heart-healthy. I will not do this with toxic people unless I absolutely have to. I know my limits. All the same, if a toxic person insists on hanging out with me, and I feel the burden to accept that person's invitation, I don't invite that person to my house, nor will I go to his or her house. I ask to meet in a public place, like a restaurant or a park. This is because as an empathetic person, I try to avoid getting too comfortable around toxic people. Environments matter to prophetic people! A restaurant ensures that we can't get too comfortable for too long! A park is even better! It allows me to invest an hour or two into hanging out with that person, and then escaping when I start feeling drained. At the same time, I'm not home to empty out my closet. This means I'm potting the plant outside of its natural environment! In other words, I'm bringing that cousin outside of her comfort zone and I'm coming outside my comfort zone. We're coming onto neutral territory. This will make us more cognizant about what we say. Again, you have to know your wiring! You have to be more strategic than the devil himself!

As for gossip and slander, if this is something you've wrestled with in the past, please know that it's created the environment you're in or the environments that you once found yourself in. It set the tone for your relationships, friendships and your career path. This is something you have to renounce and wrestle down. One tool I used to diffuse gossipers is this—I insist that we pray for the person he or she is talking about. For example, look at the dialogue below. Note, this is not a conversation I've actually had; it's just an example:

> **Cousin:** Girl, did you hear about what happened to Charlotte?
> **Me:** No, I didn't. Is she okay?
> **Cousin:** I can't believe you haven't heard! Her boyfriend kicked her out of the house! He caught her cheating on him with his first cousin! And they said, this isn't the first time. Last year ….
> **Me:** Oh, that's sad. I feel bad for the both of them.

Real quick, bow your head. I want to pray for the both of them. Father God, we come before you on behalf of …

After this, I would pray for their hearts to heal, for them to find the love of God and for them to find peace. This is a SUREFIRE way to diffuse a gossiper! They hate this!

Just remember this—your words will set the tone for your environment. Your heart will set the stage for your words. Guard your heart, and be mindful of the words that you speak. Place a boundary around your lips, and anytime you come across people who are masters at getting you to lower your guards, distance yourself from those people until you are strong enough, mature enough and wise enough to affect the atmosphere, instead of being affected by it. All the same, remember, you need to know your wiring. This will help you to be more strategic than you are reactive.

FALSE BOUNDARIES

Anytime a fence is erected, it has to be established on a solid rock. Without the foundation, the fence has a form, but no power. The same is true for false boundaries. False boundaries are works, declarations and rules that have not been established on the foundation of understanding. Knowledge is the fence that surrounds any given system; it is the wall in our belief system that separates the conscious mind from the subconscious mind. The conscious mind deals with what we are presently aware of, for example, you are consciously aware of the sounds playing in the background, the book you're reading right now and how you feel. All of the information that surrounds you every day goes directly to your conscious mind, but to get to the subconscious, which is where the heart is located, that information has to be permitted in by you through belief. The moment you believe something, it goes from your conscious to your subconscious. Other rivers or routes into your belief system are:

1. Trauma
2. False doctrines
3. Music

Whatever information you allow into your belief system will directly affect your life because it becomes a river that you source from. God told us to guard our subconscious or, better yet, our hearts. In other words, get understanding.

Without understanding, knowledge is easily moved aside. For example, most believers know that the Bible teaches against fornication, so there are singles who have declared themselves to be abstinent, and while this is great, their abstinence is nothing but a fence (knowledge) without a foundation (understanding). If I know that sex outside of marriage is wrong, but I don't understand why it's wrong, my knowledge will have a lot of give to it. Knowledge is the fence itself, but the concrete foundation of knowledge is understanding. Notice the words "under" and "standing." This deals with positioning. Understanding is the structure that holds knowledge up; this is what gives knowledge its power. It goes without saying, the more knowledge you have, the more understanding you'll need. Wisdom, on the other hand, is what holds knowledge together. We need all three (wisdom, knowledge and understanding) in order for a boundary to solidify. Any boundaries that have not been solidified are easily pushed down or pushed aside.

Again, a lot of believers claim abstinence, but they lack understanding. In truth, many of these believers are essentially saying to Satan that they are fed up with the types of men that he's been tossing at them. (Please note that they don't pray to Satan, but their choices serve as communication to him that they are fed up with him making promises to them, only for them to be left disappointed.)They are tired of being cheated on, used, rejected and abandoned, so basically, what they are having is a standoff with Satan. In short, they are pretty much just rioting and protesting his ways by closing their legs. Satan then responds by sending love interests their way. If he sends the same type of men, for example, that he's been sending, these women will continue their standoff. They'll keep proclaiming to be abstinent, all the while, dating his sons. (The same is true for men, of course; this is just an example.) Eventually, Satan responds by sending them someone who is different; this is someone who appears to be better than the last few guys. He will send a guy who has more money, more structure and more relational longevity than the last few guys. (A generational curse often manifests itself as a person being able to go so far in a relationship; either the person cannot stay committed past six months or the person typically bails out of a relationship after a child is born. This is a pattern of behavior that has been passed down from one generation to the next.) If a woman is used to being dumped after six months, and she meets a man with more relational longevity—a man who tells her that his last two relationships, for example, lasted five years, she will see him as a rarity. Of course, this means that she'll attempt to solidify or establish their relationship because she'll be deceived into believing that she can get him to stick with her for the rest of his life. This is when she'll end her protest against Satan and his systems; this is when she'll toss abstinence (or her claim thereof) out the window and she'll engage in a sexual relationship with the guy. She'll even go as far as to put on a theatrical performance for the guy by crying and claiming to feel bad about having fallen into sexual sin. This is to guilt-trip him into marrying her.

Abstinence was just another tool in her bag.

A lot of women (believers included) have a bag of wiles;
these are the behaviors, mind-games and manipulations
they engage in every time they enter into a relationship.
They use these tools because they want to get married, but
they lack the knowledge needed to be wives. When they've
tried everything in their bags of tricks, and they hear about
abstinence, they will oftentimes elect to add abstinence to
this proverbial bag. In other words, this is a false boundary.
In most cases, the types of men that they ordinarily date
don't usually come across women who claim to be abstinent,
so in an attempt to stand out and provoke the hunter in these
guys, they start using what they've learned about abstinence
to finally get their way. They may have went to church and
met couples who have openly testified about remaining
abstinent until married, and because they don't understand
true, Godly love, they assume that the men married those
women ONLY because they didn't give into their sexual
demands. They believe that the husbands of these women
had gotten so sexually frustrated or so sexually curious that
they finally gave in and married them. Having never tried this
approach, they decide to add it to their bag of tricks. These
women can go for years without having sex; they will ignore
their desire to have sex because they have a bigger issue to
feed, and that is their idolatry. Again, every time Satan
throws the same types of men he's been throwing at them,
they will date the guys but refuse to have sex with them; that
is, until Satan finally sends someone who's different their

way. Satan then responds by sending them someone who appears to be better, who appears to be more mature or has more relational longevity. For the most part, they won't hurriedly give in when they meet these guys; they'll continue to claim abstinence, all the while or inviting the guys over to their homes while no one else is there, going over to these guys' homes while no one else is there just to tease them. Satan knows how to play this game well, after all, it is one of his wiles. So, the men in question dig deep into their bags of tricks and pull out their own wiles. A man like this, for example, may suddenly stop calling a woman, and every time she calls or texts him, he'll claim to be busy or sleepy. Realizing that she's in the process of being abandoned again, the woman then begins to rethink her position. She may respond with a text message saying, "Can you come over tonight? I don't want to be alone. I'm scared because there has been a series of break-ins in my neighborhood." Make no mistake about it, she's not afraid. Break-ins are commonplace in her neighborhood, but this is just her way of letting him know that she's ready to give him the sin offering he's requiring to remain active in her life. Of course, he'll respond by calling her, and when he does, she'll notice a different tone in his voice. He doesn't sound disinterested anymore; instead, he will pretend to be concerned. "I get off at 7:30. I'll be there around nine. I have to stop by my house to get some clothes," he says. Later that evening when he arrives, she will continue to put on a performance. "You can sleep on the couch," she says. He will agree, knowing that she's simply trying to ease her way into the encounter because she doesn't want to look easy. It has to appear to have been an accident or a decision made in the heat of a moment; this way, her teary-eyed performance after the sexual encounter will appear to be authentic. Of course, the two will either engage in full-on sex or the woman may decide that she wants to engage only in sexual favors; for her, to serves three purposes:

1. It allows her to continue claiming to be abstinent, and by abstinent, she means that she hasn't been penetrated vaginally for a series of months or years. In many cases, she has told a group of people that she is abstinent or she may even have a ministerial platform centered around sexual purity.

2. It gives the man a snippet, a sample or a preview of what he will have should he marry her. This allows her to show off her sexual prowess; this is her way of saying to him, "Trust me, I know what I'm doing."

3. To keep the man from breaking up with her to pursue someone who's willing to engage him sexually. The goal here is to establish or strengthen the soul tie between the two.

4. To keep the man from cheating on her.

5. To satisfy her lust.

Of course, if she engages in sexual favors, unbeknownst to her, she is NOT abstinent because she has not been abstaining from sex. Relationships like these are built on and centered around pure, unadulterated idolatry. The foundation of fornication 98 percent of the time is idolatry. And of course, most babes in Christ are going to establish false boundaries because they don't yet have understanding, and this is what leads them into a series of relationships with narcissistic people. But as they mature, their boundaries will begin to solidify. Howbeit, anytime a mature or seasoned believer engages in these practices, the believer is simply rebelling. This is oftentimes because the believer has never dated someone without introducing sex into the relationship at some point. In other words, that individual does not know how to date or court with his/her clothes on. This is similar to purchasing a burger, fries and a soda. Most of us associate sodas with burgers and fries, so regardless of what other beverages a restaurant offers, we habitually order a soda anytime we order a hamburger with fries. People treat relationships the same way. They've never had a relationship without sex being involved, so regardless of how long they've been in the faith, they will continue to have sex outside of marriage or perform sexual favors anytime they find themselves in a relationship that lasts a certain amount of time. Again, these are false boundaries; they have the form or appearances of boundaries, but they have no power.

Of course, false boundaries aren't just limited to sex. They are cheap structures erected in every area where we lack understanding. When you lack understanding, it's okay to have boundaries that have not been solidified by understanding, but to secure yourself, you have to be accountable to someone. For example, you can say to someone who is mature, "I'm trying to practice abstinence, but I don't fully understand abstinence or how to navigate this season of my life, so I need to be accountable to someone. Will you be my accountability partner?" And please understand that the person does NOT have to be accountable to you. All the same, you have to be consistently accountable; you can't hide what you decide are small details from the person. False accountability is a false boundary. False honor is another false boundary. False boundaries are oftentimes established when a believer agrees to follow what everyone else is doing without attempting to understand why they do it. And again, if you are a new believer or you're immature in the faith, following people who are doing what the Bible says is a GREAT idea, however, you should always seek to understand why they do what they do so that your followship does not become manipulation. Back in 2006, when I didn't understand abstinence, I tried to follow the rules and do the right thing, but because I lacked understanding, my abstinence was just a smoke screen and a joke. It lasted for about five months. I was going through a divorce at the time and trying to navigate my new reality. So, I phoned a friend and asked her to be my accountability partner. The problem with this was, she was struggling with fornication herself! So, we agreed to hold each other accountable, but that ended up being short-lived.

Look at every area of your life, and ask yourself this, "Are those boundaries real or do I lack understanding?" If you lack understanding, buy or rent some books! Also, read articles online about whatever it is that you do not understand. For example, if you don't understand honor, study it. Don't create false boundaries by publicly professing to honor your leaders, only to find yourself leaving your church when the spirit of offense comes to test those boundaries. Find some great books and video teachings about honor, and study until you fully understand what honor is and why it is important. You also need to understand the penalties of dishonor and see examples of people who've benefited from the honor system versus people who've fallen into the traps of dishonor. The goal here is to learn the patterns of God and the patterns of the enemy; this way, you'll be able to accurately predict the outcome of a particular behavior. For example, narcissistic relationships or relationships centered around idolatry are now a science to me. This is because of the knowledge I've extracted from wrestling with a particular spirit or stronghold over the course of time AND from me counseling people who've taken the same route. Every highway leads to a particular place; no highway changes its destination. It simply serves as a bridge to get us from one place to another. The same is true regarding choices and beliefs. They are all bridges that lead to a particular outcome CONSISTENTLY! So, if I've seen four people drink from a specific cup, and they'll all fallen dead within minutes, it goes without saying that I'm not going to think for one second that the fifth person is going to survive drinking from that same glass. No. I'll try to get that person to avoid that cup altogether. But if I'm unable to stop the individual, I have to sit and watch them savor what's in the cup, all the while knowing what's about to become of them. Someone will argue, "A poisonous snake bit Paul and the people thought he was going to die, but instead, he shook the snake off in a fire!" Paul was within the confines of God's will! Paul was not in sin gambling with his soul (mind, will and emotions), so this argument does not apply to a sinful event orchestrated by a rebelling Christian. Again, make sure that every area of your life is surrounded by boundaries, and make sure that you solidify those boundaries by getting all of the understanding you need to secure the knowledge that you have. You can do it! All of Heaven is rooting for you!

THE MAKING OF BOUNDARIES

Again, I like to think of mercy as a leash and even a lease. It is a space in time that Satan gets to hold the end of that leash, tugging away at your potential and your identity. Once you learn to walk in the spirit and not the flesh, you will separate yourself from your fleshly desires, thus, unlocking your potential and your God-given identity. So, the lease is just the time allotted for you to tug on that leash until you (not your flesh) breaks away from it. Your flesh is like a rabid pit bull; it is not a friend of your spirit man. The two of them are contrary to one another. So, when you're feeding your flesh, you're feeding your inner-me or your enemy. It will grow and grow until it's big enough to consume you. In other words, you'd find yourself pretty much filled with or addicted to whatever issue you've been feeding. Mercy is the leash that holds those pit bulls in place; God's mercy keeps you from being consumed by the very things that you feed. Again, mercy is an extension of grace; it is not God's compliance with your rebellion. It is His way of saying, "I understand why you do the things that you do; it's only because you don't know Me. So, I'm giving you the space and the resources to get to know Me better, because if you know Me, you'll love Me. And if you love Me, you'll keep My commandments." What are His commandments again? Jesus answered this in Matthew 22:37-40. "Jesus said unto him, Thou shalt love the Lord thy God with all thy heart, and with all thy soul, and with all thy mind. This is the first and great commandment. And the second is like unto it, Thou shalt love thy neighbor as thyself. On these two commandments hang all the law and the prophets." Love is the answer! When we love the Lord with all of our hearts and soul (mind, will and emotions), we will truly learn to love ourselves. I'm not talking about this counterfeit love that's popular today, where people take hiatuses away from other people, try to reinvent themselves, post excessive amounts of photos of themselves on social media and claim to be new people, after all, that's just trauma masquerading itself as love. I'm talking about genuine to-the-core love. True, wholehearted, God-established love makes you want to worship the Lord with more intensity, give Him more of your time and more of your resources. That's self-love manifesting itself! It's the fruit of true love! When we love ourselves, we can truly love our neighbors as we love ourselves. God will give you the wisdom, knowledge and understanding you need to outgrow whatever issues you've been feeding. He'll place mentors in your life, point you to a church and provide you with a Bible. He'll also make books, webinars and teachings available for you to consume; this way, you can stop feeding your lusts and place that flesh of yours on the altar to be sacrificed (Romans 12:1) time and time again until it finally and fully submits to the Word. Howbeit, if you reject Him by rejecting the knowledge of Him, you may find yourself being consumed by the pit bulls (flesh) that you've been feeding. These pit bulls or pitfalls include perversion and pride. People who are turned over to reprobate minds find themselves overcome by their lusts with no help from God whatsoever. Romans 1:28-32 details what it's like to have a reprobate mind. "And even as they did not like to retain God in their knowledge, God gave them over to a reprobate mind, to do those things which are not convenient; being filled with all unrighteousness, fornication, wickedness, covetousness, maliciousness; full of envy, murder, debate, deceit, malignity; whisperers, backbiters, haters of God, despiteful, proud, boasters, inventors of evil things, disobedient to parents, without understanding, covenant breakers, without natural affection, implacable, unmerciful: Who knowing the judgment of God, that they which commit such things are worthy of death, not only do the same, but have pleasure in them that do them." Notice the keywords here are "filled with" and "full of." This means that all of the pitfalls (issues) will be unleashed on the person who loves those issues.

While the repercussions of sin don't always materialize themselves instantaneously, they have no choice but to manifest at some point. This is because the Word of God cannot and will not return to Him void. Again, it's impossible for God to lie! The blood of Jesus wiped away our sins, but fornication, murder, rape, lying, stealing and every other loveless act did not cease to be wrong after Jesus was hung on the cross. They are still choices that provoke God's Word to respond. This is because sin is a part of a larger system; it is the inner workings of the kingdom of darkness, and it allows Satan to reproduce his fruit in our lives and in the lives of those closest to us. It also allows him to kill, steal and destroy because sin is his domain. When we flirt with his kingdom, we sow seeds into darkness—seeds that we ultimately have to reap. One of the laws instituted by God and spoken of by Apostle Paul is listed in Galatians 6:7. It states, "Be not deceived; God is not mocked: for whatsoever a man soweth, that shall he also reap." Remember, the Bible was not written for the unbeliever, but for the believer. This means that God is speaking directly to us, the Church! This puts to rest the idea that there are no longer any repercussions for sin. Quite the contrary! To whom much is given, much is required; when God gives us His Word, He gives us a greater standard to live by. If you'll look at the history of Christians who took grace for granted, you'll see a pattern of sickness, disease, separation, dependency and premature death. The boundaries between light and darkness are still there, and we are still commanded not to cross those boundaries; yes, even if we don't understand or agree with them. God knows that because of our sin nature and lack of knowledge, we oftentimes blur the lines between right and wrong. This is what grace is for. Grace is not a condom for us to utilize whenever we want the pleasures of sin, but not the issues that sin produces. It is not a raincoat that allows us to play in the rain and not get wet. Grace simply allows us to be flawed humans, meaning, we'll make mistakes, but as long as we repent and turn away from our wicked ways, the kingdom of darkness has no jurisdiction in our lives. But if we live rebellious lives, knowing right from wrong, but choosing to be led by the lusts of our flesh, we then begin to tap into God's mercy. Grace keeps us from getting what we deserve; mercy keeps what we deserve from getting the best of us! And let me make sure I mention this—if you're struggling with issues like fornication, homosexuality, anger or anything that's displeasing to God, please don't think you've been turned over to a reprobate mind. Chances are, you're still young in the faith; yes, even if you've been in church for the majority of your life! For example, not having grown up in church, I found myself surrounded by a lot of "church folks" in my teenage years, and I remember a couple of my friends whose parents would pretty much drag me to church with them when I was a teenager. And while they were great people, they weren't mature in the faith. I was a perverted teen who loved the world, but I was able to recognize whenever a person didn't practice what they preached. I learned young that religious people often used "church language" to appear holy, but you could not find any shred of holiness in their lives. They went to church, read their Bibles and said "hallelujah" or "glory to His name" every few seconds. They quoted scriptures and did some of the fanciest footwork I'd ever seen, but they didn't respect the boundaries between right and wrong; they lived on the wrong side of those boundaries, and to be honest with you, I was such a dark person that I found their hypocrisy to be amusing, if not funny. I would often joke with my friends about how religious their parents were. But were they hell bound? No! They were trying to win a soul (me) for the Lord. They were just immature. Immature believers are oftentimes extremely religious; they can be abrasive, judgmental and prideful. Those fruits signify that they are immature or still growing into their identities in Christ. Were they hypocrites? Yep! But this is because they didn't understand the Word that they preached! Immature believers know scriptures, but they don't know God intimately. They know church culture, but they do not understand Kingdom culture. And they often drive more people away from God than they win for Him. Telling an unbeliever to be fake is one of the quickest ways to lose that person's trust and interest. I kept falling into the snares of sin until I truly got to know God two marriages and a whole lot of heart-wounds later! Let me help you see this from another angle. In the kingdom of darkness, I was a grown woman. I was knowledgeable, bold and determined to get whatever it was that I wanted. I had mastered my sins, and those sins had mastered me. I knew how to extract whatever it was I wanted whenever I wanted it. I was still talented and skilled, but my gifts were perverted. But in the Kingdom of God, I was but a babe. I was unlearned, fearful and unsure. Because of this, I kept leaning to what I knew; I kept relying on the world's system to validate and affirm me. I was still interested in the world's men and there was no way I was going to stop gratifying my flesh. I loved to drink, fornicate and rebel against any and everything that kept me from having fun. But there was a seed in me that needed watering. That seed caused me to hunger and thirst after righteousness. It was a seed that my great-grandmother had planted before she'd passed away when I was four or five-years old. It was a seed that my dad had watered every time he'd come into my bedroom and read the Bible to me and my brother (we shared a room). So, I was drawn to people who practiced what they preached, not out of religiousness because I detested religious folks. I was drawn to people who truly loved the Lord. I could easily tell the difference based on the look in their eyes when they spoke about Him and the way they ministered to me about my lifestyle. Some of them were hard on me, and get this, I wasn't mad at them about it BECAUSE their lifestyles reflected what they preached. Some of them were patient with me, but none of them were my personal mentors. I just saw them around at work or in my neighborhood, and I watched them closely because I admired them. I had never seen an example of what it meant to establish a boundary and enforce it; that is until I got hired at a local retail store. I ended up being under an assistant who was on fire for God, and she was a young woman; she was only 24 years old! I was around 19 or 20. She'd piqued my interest when she'd told me that she was a 24-year old virgin. I couldn't believe what I was hearing. I didn't even think it was possible to be 24 and still a virgin. So, I watched her, asked a bunch of questions and went out of my way to win favor with her. I didn't do this for a raise. I did it because I genuinely wanted to know more about God, and I wanted her to mentor me. I knew she couldn't do this offsite, but I figured that if I did what I was supposed to do and more, she'd share more of her wisdom with me, and she did. I laugh because she didn't realize she was unofficially mentoring me, so she would sometimes get annoyed with my colorful questions, but I wanted to learn how to be the type of woman she was so much so that I would ignore her frowns just to get to the revelation. Eventually, she caught on and began to pour a little more into me, and she began to rebuke me a little more. In her short time as my assistant manager, she had pretty much served as my very first pastor. My fascination with her grew when I saw her literally practice what she'd been preaching. She had a fiancé who also worked as an assistant manager, and he'd been transferred to another store in a nearby state. I hadn't heard her mention him in a while, so I asked about him. When she told me they'd broke up, I was shocked. Who would want to break up with a 24-year old virgin who loved the Lord and was building her career? I couldn't even fathom that such a man existed, especially when that woman was a beautiful woman, both inside and out. She didn't look surprised by my question, nor did she appear to be sad. She told me that they'd broken up because he wanted to stay at her house. He was going to be in town one weekend, and he'd tried to invite himself into her house. She told him no. She told him that he'd have to get a hotel for himself. She wasn't about to put herself in a position where she could not only compromise her purity, but she also wanted to refrain from the appearance of evil. They'd argued about this, and she ended the relationship because the guy didn't want to respect her choice to remain pure. This guy was handsome, well-spoken and he seemed to be climbing the ladder of success as well. She'd given me my very first glimpse of Godly confidence. This began my journey towards a true relationship with God, after all, I only needed to see that it was possible to be a non-hypocritical

Christian.

Not long after that, I found myself having a drunken conversation about salvation while driving back to my city from a club. The club was more than an hour away, and a friend of mine would often accompany me to this club every Thursday night. We'd party hard, get drunk and then drive home around two or three in the morning. We'd then have to get back up around 5:30 the next morning to get ready for work, since we were also co-workers. On this particular night, I remember being so drunk that I almost drove us into a forest. I didn't notice the curve in the road; I just saw the pathway between the trees and assumed it was a road. Moments before hitting a tree, my friend started screaming at me. "Tiffany, what are you doing?!" I laughed as I realized my mistake. We got back on the road and not long after that, she broke the silence again. "Tiffany, we gotta stop doing this," she said. "We gotta give our lives to Christ. I've been thinking a lot lately and I need to get my life together." Those words were refreshing to me, even though I was half-drunk. I'd been having the same thoughts. She then told me about a church her aunt attended and we both agreed to go there the following Sunday. Three Sundays later, I got up and joined the church. A few months to a year later, I renounced clubs and bars. Like most baby Christians (if not all), I struggled with sexual sin and other issues. My boundaries were weak in some areas, non-existent in other areas and fluid in some areas. As my pastor preached the Word, I found myself feeling extremely convicted Sunday after Sunday, but here's the surprise—I wasn't offended at all! This is why I don't agree with the ever-growing belief that to win a soul, you have to dance around that person's feelings. It's not true! People who truly want Christ will allow themselves to be offended; people who want to manipulate and control other people will pretend to want Christ just to get whatever it is that they want. I remember my pastor preaching a sermon and something he said jumped off his lips and pierced through my wounded soul. He said, "The word whoremonger has nothing to do with the amount of men a woman sleeps with. Biblically speaking, a whore was and still is a woman who has sex outside of marriage." I sat there and thought to myself, "Oh my goodness, I'm a whore!" That was a label that I'd gone out of my way to avoid wearing. I thought a whore was a woman who slept with multiple men at one time or within a small window of time. I thought a whore was someone who slept with someone else's man or a woman who slept with men she didn't know. All of my "activities" had been done under the girlfriend title, and I would be monogamous to the man I was with when I was in a relationship. Outside of a relationship, I had what I called a "splakavelli." I'd gotten that term from a popular song that had encouraged women to have a side-dude. The video starred one of the finest men in the world to me at that time, and that was actor Shemar Moore. To me, a "splak" was a handsome, successful and well-spoken man who didn't mind having a no-strings-attached sexual relationship with a woman who was in between relationships or a woman who wanted to pay her beau back for his indiscretions. The "splak" I chose for myself met all of those requirements and then some. He was extremely handsome, well-built, very successful and educated. And he didn't mind being my dirty secret; actually, he loved the idea (obviously). And there I was sitting in church, learning that the whole time I'd used my "splak" so that I wouldn't become a "ho," I'd been fooling myself. Now, some believers and leaders would say, "That wasn't a nice thing for your pastor to say, especially on a platform." Listen, I didn't need a nice pastor, I needed someone to tell me the truth! I wasn't mad at him for saying this, and neither was my friend. Our mouths dropped and we looked at each other. Honestly, I'm pretty sure we had a good laugh about it after service, but in that moment, I realized that I was going to have to create some boundaries—first for myself, and then, for every person who entered my life. I was going to also have to stop calling my "splak" every time I found myself in between relationships. And it took me several years after this to finally love God enough to remain abstinent, and Lord knows, I tried and failed many times. I kept trying to modify my behavior, not realizing that without knowing God intimately, my attempts to "be" a Christian woman would be nothing more than me performing for God. Now, don't get me wrong, I completely and wholeheartedly believe that every single woman should practice abstinence. To date, I've been abstinent for six years; this is a feat I NEVER would have thought I could have accomplished, especially after failing so many times. But again, I am all for immature men and women intentionally refraining from sexual immorality and every other work of the flesh. I encourage this even before their hearts change, however, I'm not shocked when a babe in Christ falls into one of these snares, nor do I think the believer is damned to hell. Babies, when they are learning to walk, fall a lot. They keep doing this until they learn to stand on their own.

But how do you make boundaries? Think of it like setting up a fence around your property. First and foremost, if you've decided to set up a fence, it's because you're trying to keep something out of your yard or you're trying keep a pet or a child in your yard. This is your why. Next, you have to establish or know where your property lines end, versus where your neighbors' property lines begin. You do this through zoning. In short, you can't set boundaries in another person's life; you can only establish them in your own life. For example, you can say to your boyfriend that you don't believe in sex outside of marriage, but this doesn't mean that you'll be able to keep him from having sex with other people. If he violates your trust, it is your responsibility to respond to the violation. If you forgive him, that's great, but you must understand that forgiving him doesn't guarantee that he'll be faithful in the future. If you end the relationship, that's great, but you can't monitor his life or who he's seeing. Your job is to guard your heart, not his. You are the one who decides what's acceptable (legal) or unacceptable (illegal) in your life. Again, you have to establish where your property lines end versus where someone else's property lines begin. Next, you have to count the costs. Think about purchasing an actual fence. You'd have to get some of the employees from the company you're contracting with to come over to measure your property; this way, they can determine how much fence you'll need. This is one of the steps they'll need to take in order to give you a quote for the work you want done. Another step they'd have to take is to get you to determine what type of fencing you want. Do you want something that's attractive, but ineffective? This is a front or the appearance of boundaries, but not the actual presence of boundaries. Do you want something that's inexpensive? This is a settlement offer. It's when the enemy realizes that you're about to win, so he offers you a settlement. For example, if you've been praying for a Godly spouse, and you have been chasing the heart of God, getting your deliverance and studying the Word, the enemy will soon realize that you are about to break a generational curse. So, he'll offer you the man of your dreams, but the catch is—the guy's not saved or he's a five-percenter. Nevertheless, his parents are pastors, so the enemy will reason with you that he will eventually turn his life around because it's in his blood. But consider this—maybe, his parents aren't saved; instead, they're religious, narcissistic and abusive. Howbeit, they are pastoring a church and they are great at looking the part. In other words, what you're wanting him to return to is probably worse than what he's running from! Then again, do you want a fence that's both attractive and effective? Of course, the contractors will show you a brochure so that you can decide. The type of fencing you use simply means the type of boundaries you want to set. After all, some people like false boundaries because they have no intentions to change. Again, they want the appearance of having boundaries, but they are not interested in truly setting boundaries. Then again, there are some people out there who are hungry and desperate for a change to occur in their lives, and these people are willing to establish some hard boundaries in their lives to get the results they want; that is, to keep wild animals out of their lives, and to keep themselves from roaming into the wilderness and finding another potential ex to entertain for a few months or a few years. Next, you have to count the cost! Again, let's think of an actual fence. Once you choose the fence type you want, the company will send you an estimate. You will then determine if you're willing to make that big of a sacrifice to get what you want or if you just want to cut corners to save money. In other words, this will determine how desperate you are to be free! For example, whenever I started establishing hard boundaries around myself, because of the levels of toxicity in my family, I knew that I'd lose my relationship with the large majority of them. This is because many of them see boundaries as control or the proof that you think you're better than them, so they rebel loudly and violently against anything that looks like order. Nevertheless, I counted the cost and decided that I'd rather have peace on every side than to be surrounded by family members and chaos. This isn't to say that I don't love my family because I do! I simply established boundaries around myself, and in order for me to have a relationship with anyone, family or not, that person has to respect my boundaries. And finally, you have to pay the price. This is where most people end their journeys. They'll get this far, declaring that they are willing to pay the price, only to find themselves longing for a sense of belonging. This is where most believers turn back and return to their bondage, hoping to find another way to freedom that does not involve them offending the people they love. But please understand that setting and enforcing boundaries in your own personal life is necessary if you want to live a long, productive and happy life! All the same, bound people hate boundaries, so it goes without saying that they will rebel anytime they feel limited by a boundary. Removing your boundaries to keep the peace in your family does NOT benefit your family; it simply allows the toxicity to travel to another generation; that is, until someone is born who's willing to count the costs and pay the price! And by paying the price, I mean that the person is willing to speak with the family (in love) about the issues present. That person is willing to do what it takes to get the healing and deliverance he or she will need to finally break the curse that the previous generation refused to confront. That person is willing to be persecuted, ostracized and ignored by the family simply because he or she refuses to embrace toxicity, and because the person has truly chosen to embrace Jesus Christ and not religion. This will undoubtedly cause a domino effect to take place, because many of the younger people in the family will actually begin to follow suit. This is because younger people are oftentimes not bound by the memories, traditions and customs of the former generation. Consequently, they don't share their beliefs. Whenever they see a family member who is bold enough to go against the grain of dysfunction, they feel empowered to do the same. This is how curses are broken!

THE PURPOSE OF BOUNDARIES

The reason God created boundaries was so that His will could be done. What is the will of God? Jeremiah 29:11-14 reads, "For I know the thoughts that I think toward you, saith the LORD, thoughts of peace, and not of evil, to give you an expected end. Then shall ye call upon me, and ye shall go and pray unto me, and I will hearken unto you. And ye shall seek me, and find *me*, when ye shall search for me with all your heart. And I will be found of you, saith the LORD: and I will turn away your captivity, and I will gather you from all the nations, and from all the places whither I have driven you, saith the LORD; and I will bring you again into the place whence I caused you to be carried away captive.

From the beginning of time, God instituted boundaries; yes, even before the Earth was created. We all know the story of Lucifer. He wanted something that wasn't his. He coveted the throne and power of God for himself. At that time, Lucifer was one of God's angels. Consider how God addressed him in Ezekiel 28:13-19. "Thou hast been in Eden the garden of God; every precious stone was thy covering, the sardius, topaz, and the diamond, the beryl, the onyx, and the jasper, the sapphire, the emerald, and the carbuncle, and gold: the workmanship of thy tabrets and of thy pipes was prepared in thee in the day that thou wast created. Thou art the anointed cherub that covereth; and I have set thee so: thou wast upon

127

the holy mountain of God; thou hast walked up and down in the midst of the stones of fire. Thou wast perfect in thy ways from the day that thou wast created, till iniquity was found in thee. By the multitude of thy merchandise they have filled the midst of thee with violence, and thou hast sinned: therefore I will cast thee as profane out of the mountain of God: and I will destroy thee, O covering cherub, from the midst of the stones of fire. Thine heart was lifted up because of thy beauty, thou hast corrupted thy wisdom by reason of thy brightness: I will cast thee to the ground, I will lay thee before kings, that they may behold thee. Thou hast defiled thy sanctuaries by the multitude of thine iniquities, by the iniquity of thy traffick; therefore will I bring forth a fire from the midst of thee, it shall devour thee, and I will bring thee to ashes upon the earth in the sight of all them that behold thee. All they that know thee among the people shall be astonished at thee: thou shalt be a terror, and never shalt thou be any more."

Lucifer crossed a boundary with God. Like humans, angels have the freedom to exercise their own will; they are not given to instinct. Therefore, Lucifer had the ability to choose to do right or wrong. He chose to create another system, one that opposed the will of God. The Bible calls him the "father of all lies." Now, God is Truth; we understand this, and He is our Father. The opposite or opposing force of truth, of course, is a lie. So, Lucifer began to create his own kingdom and his own system, but every kingdom needs rulers and inhabitants. Therefore, he deceived a third of the angels that were in Heaven (see Revelation 12:4); this is why he is called a liar and a thief. The Kingdom of God's system was moving in one direction, but Lucifer chose to oppose the will and the works of God. When you oppose the will of God, you become an opponent of God. An opponent fights against a system, rather than working with it. Imagine a machine with gears and wheels moving clockwise. Now imagine someone causing a few of the wheels to move counterclockwise. If this were to happen, a loud sound would emit from the machine, and we'd see sparks just before the machine either jammed or went up in flames and destroyed itself. Thankfully for us, God's will is way bigger than any and every angel or living thing, so Satan's will was not big enough or powerful enough to stop the will of God. (Think of a small wheel or gear moving in the opposite direction of a huge wheel or gear. The small wheel doesn't stand a chance.) Instead, Lucifer brought a curse upon himself and the angels that followed his lead. In that moment, Lucifer had become a ruler, therefore, there was no place found for him anymore in Heaven (one house cannot have two fathers or two rulers ruling over it). He was given the name Satan, which means "adversary" and evicted from Heaven, along with the angels who were now in agreement with him.

Lucifer had crossed a boundary and an instant transformation took place. What was once a beautiful angel had become an ugly devil. A creature that once had an angelic voice now made a repulsive sound. To add insult to injury, he soon realized that running his own kingdom was nothing like he'd imagined it would be. After all, anything that is established outside the will of God is accursed. His angels weren't happy. They'd lost their splendor as well. Nothing he did prospered; everything he did failed.

One day, Satan looked towards the Garden of Eden and saw a beautiful woman, clothed in the glory of God. She was everything that he once was. She was the picture of perfection! At this time, Satan hadn't been banned from Eden. (Note: contrary to popular belief, Eden was not in Heaven. Heaven is the dwelling place of God. Eden was and is here on Earth.) Satan walked over to the woman, after all, he wanted her to oppose God's will just as he had. He wanted something so precious to God to partner with him and his kingdom, but to attain this, he had to do to Eve what he'd done with a third of God's angels—he told her a lie. To make it more palatable, he seasoned the lie with a few facts and offered it to her. The father of all lies opened his mouth and began to speak the language of his kingdom to Eve. She listened to him intently, and before long, she found herself standing on the right side of a boundary staring at another system. According to Satan, in his system, she'd be a ruler; she'd be like God and she'd know all things. Moments later, Eve reached past the boundary and shook hands with the devil; in that moment, she'd sinned against God. She then became sin; she hadn't just sinned, but she became a sinner or an opposer of the will of God. She brought her sin into the Garden with her and handed it to her husband.

The present boundary had been placed there to keep the couple in the will of God. All the same, the boundaries that God has given us are there to protect us and to keep us in the will of God. God's will allows us to plug into Heaven's system and reap the blessings that Christ has afforded us through His precious shed blood. You see, because of sin, we were not able to access the presence of God. Only the high priest of the Jews could go into His presence. But when Jesus died for us, the veil was torn, meaning, the boundaries were lifted. Matthew 27:50-53 details this moment. "Jesus, when he had cried again with a loud voice, yielded up the ghost. And, behold, the veil of the temple was rent in twain from the top to the bottom; and the earth did quake, and the rocks rent; and the graves were opened; and many bodies of the saints which slept arose, and came out of the graves after his resurrection, and went into the holy city, and appeared unto many." Only the high priest had been permitted to enter the Holy of Holies once a year and go past the veil, but the moment the veil was rent or, better yet, torn, it signified the removal of an old system and the institution of a new one. Man could now go before God on his own. This is because Jesus is our High Priest and He makes intercession for us. The system of works was demolished and the system of grace was instituted.

Now, this needs to be emphasized once again. The veil of the temple ripped from top to bottom, allowing us to enter the presence of God—it did not tear so that we could enter sin without fear of consequence. This has to be stated and overly emphasized, especially in this generation and the ones to come because the message of grace is being misinterpreted to mean that believers can now enjoy the fruits of sin without the repercussions. There are just as many believers defending sin today as there are believers defending the Word of God, if not more! And sadly enough, we will continue to see a rise in this behavior. Defenders of righteousness are now laughed at, persecuted and labeled as religious. Defenders of sin are now revered as heroes; they are now referred to as "cool" and "down to earth." It needs to be understood that Christ did not die so that we could sin against Him! Nowadays, it is more common than we want to admit to hear believers saying, "Judge ye not, lest ye be judged!" Refusing to read the entirety of Jesus' statement in the book of Matthew. He said, "Judge not, that you be not judged. For with what judgment you judge, you shall be judged: and with what measure you measure, it shall be measured to you again. And why behold you the speck that is in your brother's eye, but consider not the beam that is in your own eye? Or how will you say to your brother, Let me pull the speck out of your eye; and, behold, a beam is in your own eye? You hypocrite, **first** cast out the beam out of your own eye; and then shall you see clearly to cast out the speck out of your brother's eye." In modern day language, what He was saying was don't be a hypocrite! This scripture is all about order; it is not our Lord and Savior telling us to turn a blind eye to sin! In 2 Timothy 4:3-4, we were warned that this time would come, and now, we are living in it. The scripture reads, "For the time will come when they will not endure sound doctrine; but after their own lusts shall they heap to themselves teachers, having itching ears; and they shall turn away their ears from the truth, and shall be turned unto fables." A fable is a short story that is told to teach a moral lesson. This means that we'll hear more fables and wise quotes than we'll hear scriptures! If only God's people knew and understood why He drew a line in the sand and told them not to cross it! It was for our protection the entire time! Nevertheless, Satan has convinced many that the forbidden fruits that shine so brightly before them will make their lives so much better; he's convinced many that God doesn't care about them, so they have to take care of themselves. But to do this, they have to partner with sin. They have to go up against the Kingdom's system to get what they want. In other words, they have to sow into his kingdom. And as always, he is a thief and a liar! Here are some reality checks that we need to publish and review everyday of our lives!

1. Whatever a man or woman sows, that shall he or she also reap. This is scriptural and the Word of God is infallible.
2. If you go into sin looking for a blessing, you are deceived. Another word that the Bible uses is blind! Think of it this way. Satan's kingdom is in darkness; God's Kingdom shines bright with His glory. If there was light in darkness, we'd all see it, right? We understand this logic because it is sensory perception. It helps us to think of a spiritual concept using natural reasoning. Let's apply this to sin. There

is no light in darkness or, better yet, you won't find a blessing in sin. You'll find devils disguising themselves as angels of light, promising to lead you to a brighter future, but they are all liars.

3. The wages of sin is death. Yes, even for believers! While we may not partake of hell's fury, we are still engaging the systems of sowing and reaping with every choice we make, every word we speak and every person we encounter.

4. Only bound people cross boundaries; that's how they got bound in the first place! Bound people hate boundaries. One of the easiest and most effective ways to test a spirit, outside of knowing the Word of God, is to watch its movement! If it moves contrary to the will and Word of God, it is a demon! For example, if you're a single woman dating a single man, and he claims to be a man after God's own heart, the way to see who or how he really is involves you staying in the will of God, remaining patient, being watchful, and last but not least, remaining prayerful. If he tries to lead you into sin, he's headed in the wrong direction! He's moving up against the Kingdom's system! "Ye shall know them by their fruits. Do men gather grapes of thorns, or figs of thistles?" (Matthew 7:16).

5. If the blind follow the blind, both will all fall into a ditch (see Matthew 15:14). The way of the wicked is as darkness: they know not at what they stumble (see Proverbs 4:19). Anyone who's heading in the wrong direction will not and cannot lead you to a good place.

Boundaries serve many purposes, but the main purpose is to protect the integrity of a system and the people who are a part of that system. For example, in Old Testament times, a woman did not choose her own husband; her father chose or approved her husband for her. Now, in the era we live in, such a gesture would be considered offensive because of our culture. Nevertheless, as barbaric as this act may sound, it actually had many benefits and it served many purposes. They were:

1. To protect the daughters from men whose families were not integral (think generational curses). Men who came from families judged to be immoral would often be immoral and/or they'd have trouble trading in the marketplace.

2. To protect the daughters from being deceived and willfully marrying men who had no moral compass. Here's the truth—God refers to women as "the weaker vessel." This isn't just a reference to our physical strength, it also ties into our emotional strength. A woman could easily be swayed by the wrong man if he said the right thing. This is still true today! But the father, being a man himself, could weigh a man's words and test them. He would require the man to give a bride's price in exchange for his daughter. The father wasn't selling his daughter, the bride price served several reasons, two of them being: (a) the daughter worked for her father. By giving her hand in marriage, the father would be losing a helping hand. The bride price was his way of recouping some of the

wages he'd lose by losing his daughter. (b) to see if the man was integral. A high bride price was enough to scare off insincere men who were simply infatuated with the women they were pursuing, but had no true long term plans for them. Yes, in those days, men like these existed. They saw women that they were attracted to and they wanted to spend the night or a few years of nights with those women. They wanted to appease their lusts, but a high bride price would often chase away scoundrels. (c). A high bride price would often help to mature a young man who was serious about marriage. He had to go and work to earn the bride price and prove that he'd be willing and able to provide for his new wife and their children. In the Jewish culture, there were good men and there were bad men, just as there are today. A father wanted to measure, weigh and test any man who asked for his daughter's hand in marriage. This is because, just like Satan thinks in generations, so does God.

3. To preserve the integrity and virginity of daughters; this way, a man who was a believer, a protector and a provider could come along and eventually marry the daughters. If a woman had sex outside of marriage, she was no longer eligible to be married in the Jewish culture. Instead, she would be labeled a whore and her family would be considered immoral, rebellious Jews who did not honor the traditions. This brings us to number three.

4. To preserve the name and integrity of the father.

Proverbs 22:1 reads, "A good name is rather to be chosen than great riches, and loving favour rather than silver and gold." For many of us, this is just another scripture that we have yet to explore the depths of, but for a Jewish man, his namesake was the most important treasure he owned. If a woman was found to not be a virgin, this would put a blemish on, not just her father's name, but everyone in that household and everyone closely affiliated with that family. Therefore, no (reasonable) Jewish father would allow his sons to marry into such a family, and the sons from that household would find it nearly impossible to find wives for themselves; that is, unless they married into another family who had a bad reputation. All the same, it would be difficult for the father to do business with any of his fellow Jews (Jewish men normally traded goods and services). Even a kiss outside of marriage could ruin a father's reputation and bring calamity and poverty upon his family for many generations to come.

5. To protect the family from public humiliation. In the Jewish culture, virgins wore certain garments and wives wore certain garments. A woman who'd had sex outside of marriage had to, in a sense, confess her sins by the clothes she wore. So, if she went into the marketplace, she would have to endure public ridicule and people treating her like she had a contagious disease.

6. To protect the daughter from being forced to marry an

evil man. Exodus 22:16 states, "And if a man entice a maid that is not betrothed, and lie with her, he shall surely endow her to be his wife." In short, if a man and a woman were found having sex, they would be forced to marry one another. This doesn't sound like a punishment for a woman who thinks she's in love, but the truth of the matter is, no integral man would go after a woman without her father's blessing. All the same, their household would be considered immoral and untrustworthy, and as such, no one would be willing to marry off their children to this family's future offspring. And again, the father would find it difficult, if not impossible, to trade in the marketplace. In other words, this would set off a generational curse that would ensure that the family remained in poverty for many generations. When this happened, families would often have to sell off their children to other families to serve as slaves. Women would be considered maidservants and sons, of course, would be considered servants. Let's look at Old Testament law regarding this matter. Exodus 21:2-11 states, "When you buy a Hebrew slave, he shall serve six years, and in the seventh he shall go out free, for nothing. If he comes in single, he shall go out single; if he comes in married, then his wife shall go out with him. If his master gives him a wife and she bears him sons or daughters, the wife and her children shall be her master's, and he shall go out alone. But if the slave plainly says, 'I love my master, my wife, and my children; I will not go out free,' then his master shall bring him to God, and he shall bring him to the door or the doorpost. And his master shall bore his ear through with an awl, and he shall be his slave forever. "When a man sells his daughter as a slave, she shall not go out as the male slaves do. If she does not please her master, who has designated her for himself, then he shall let her be redeemed. He shall have no right to sell her to a foreign people, since he has broken faith with her. If he designates her for his son, he shall deal with her as with a daughter. If he takes another wife to himself, he shall not diminish her food, her clothing, or her marital rights. And if he does not do these three things for her, she shall go out for nothing, without payment of money." So, as you can see, this could have generational repercussions.

Again, these were just a few of the benefits of a father choosing his daughter's husband in the Old Testament. The father, in a sense, drew boundaries around his family and his own name. He understood that a blemish on his name didn't just affect him, it would affect his family for many, many generations to come.

As time progressed, we started seeing an increase in fatherless homes, an increase in fornication, an increase of poverty and an increase of crime. This is what happens when the boundaries drawn by fathers begin to fade away.

This is what happens when the people are so sin-sick that they are no longer of a sober mind; they begin to blur the lines between right and wrong, and anytime a boundary is repeatedly crossed, an accident is bound to happen. Think of the yellow lines that run down the center of our roads. This line indicates that the roads are designated for two-way traffic, meaning, while we're heading north, other drivers will use the other lane to head south. If a driver is drunk and the lines begin to blur in his sight, he may cross the line and cause an accident. Yes, even a fatal one. The lines are boundaries in the road that communicate to each driver to remain on his or her side of the road. This is why boundaries are important. They keep us from having many hardships that sin would afford us.

Understand this—every boundary that God sets was put in place to protect you. It's not there to make your life difficult or to keep you from getting whatever or whomever it is that you desire. Every boundary that is respected will lead you to a place where God's blessings are plentiful. Proverbs 10:22 says it this way, "The blessing of the LORD makes rich, and he adds no sorrow with it."

FROM ONE STATE TO ANOTHER

First and foremost, you are a multidimensional creature, meaning, your soul is comprised of many states. But what exactly is a state? The following definitions were taken from Merriam Webster for the word "state."

1. a nation or territory considered as an organized political community under one government.
2. the particular condition that someone or something is in at a specific time.
3. express something definitely or clearly in speech or writing.

Your soul is comprised of your mind, will and emotions. Your mind can be broken down into three dimensions; they are:

1. Conscious
2. Subconscious
3. Unconscious

The subconscious is the second level; this is what we refer to as the heart. This is what God told us to guard and this is where the issues of life flow from. The conscious is the outer courts of the soul; it's where information introduces itself to us before applying for a role in our hearts (subconscious). In other words, conscious is the waiting room of the soul. Howbeit, the subconscious is comprised of many states, all of which have their own unique waiting rooms. These states include:

Mental	Physical	Religious	Parental	Familial
Relational	Romantic	Sexual	Career	Financial

All of these states surround the most important aspect or dimension of who we are—our unconscious minds. This is where our souls store lost memories, trauma, etc. It also controls our breathing. This is dwelling place of our spirits. This is why we have no access to or control over this particular state. All the same, Satan cannot possess a believer because when we got saved, the Holy Spirit overshadowed our spirits, making it impossible for us to be demonically possessed, even though we can be demonically oppressed. This means a demon can get into the conscious and subconscious. His overall goal is to build a siege around the subconscious of a believer by advancing from one state to another, and then hardening the heart of the believer in an event called pride. But how does he get into these states?

1. **He engages our conscious minds.** Anything we see, taste, touch, smell or hear engages our conscious minds. And we're inundated with information, both good and bad, every single day. And every time that information presents itself to us, we will either believe it; this means that we permit it into our subconscious as a truth—we'll reject it; this means that we'll reject the entry of that information into our subconscious, and we will mentally file a report stating that the information is false or

unsubstantiated—or lastly, we could consider it. This means that we allow it to sit in the waiting room of our souls to be tried and tested later. For many people, the information that they receive is still sitting in the waiting rooms of their souls; this is why they deal with forgetfulness, anxiety and mental overwhelm. They literally have too much stuff on their minds; in other words, they need to sit down, test all of the information in their souls through study and prayer, and finally draw a conclusion.

2. **Through lack of information.** This is what we call a void. A void is a black spot on the soul that is the direct result of a lack of information. It is a soft spot on the subconscious that serves as both a door and a vacuum. In short, where there is no information, there will be an insatiable appetite for information; this appetite creates what we commonly refer to as a magnetic effect—we call this attraction. This hunger causes us to accept any information that is introduced to us, especially if that information appeals to a desire of ours. It also causes us to be attracted to the people that we are attracted to, both platonically and romantically. Please note that voids can be hereditary. For example, our parents can't teach us what they did not learn. We can go out and get that information ourselves, but we must first want it, seek it, find it, test it and embrace it.

3. **Through lack of affirmation.** Affirmation involves a true statement, emotional support, and

encouragement from someone who is notable in an individual's life. You see, sin is nothing but an identity issue; it is produced when an individual steps outside of the will of God and, of course, people do this in an attempt to "find themselves." For example, a son without a father will oftentimes try to discover who he is as an individual, why he thinks the way he thinks and why he does the things that he does. And if he doesn't have a credible man to look up to, he may look to gangs and other ungodly mediums in his attempt to not only fit in, but to receive some measure of affirmation.

4. **Through trauma.** Trauma typically happens in the area where there is a soft spot (void). Once the enemy advances into an area where there is a lack of information, he will look for ways to attack that area. For example, a young woman is traumatized in her romantic (Eros) and sexual state because of rape. While she was too immature to date, her parents gave into the pressure to let her have a boyfriend or go out on a date with that boyfriend. One day, her boyfriend picked her up and took her to the movies. After the movies, he took her by his parents' house, but neither parent was at home. Before the night was over, the young girl had been raped and she spent a great deal of time trying to understand whether she'd somehow complied with the sex or if she had truly been raped. Because she was immature and lacked information about love, romance, sex and the opposite sex, she

was traumatized in a couple of states. This may lead her to become promiscuous. What this means is that boundaries are like grass; if they are tread upon, especially more than once, they can create a trail. This trail is called a requirement. For example, before she has sex with anyone, the young woman may require the guy that she's entertaining to publicly refer to her as his girlfriend or, in some cases, she may only require dinner. This is what young men refer to as "easy." This simply means that the borders of her sexual state have little to no resistance.

5. **Through imaginations.** The Bible tells us to cast down imaginations and every high thing that exalts itself against the knowledge of God and bring into captivity every thought to the obedience of Christ. Imaginations take place in the conscious realm. Many of them are demonic commercials designed to get us to lust after lifestyles that God didn't necessarily call us to. And when these imaginations are not cast down, they will eventually find their way into our hearts, and from there, they can no longer be cast down, they have to be cast out. This is because once those imaginations go from the conscious to the subconscious, they graduate from being thoughts to beliefs. Our beliefs are the thrones in every given state; they determine who we allow to rule that area of our lives.

6. **Through rejection.** Rejection is the most common and potent weapon in Satan's arsenal. The most

powerful type of rejection is parental rejection. When the parental state is in ruins, you will find (in many cases) that every other state is in ruins. Satan then advances to other states, for example, the romantic state through the parental state, and he uses this state to enter the sexual state. He attacks each of these states until he has advanced into all of them. This allows him to build a siege wall around the unconscious mind, thus, rendering the individual a threat to himself/herself and society.

7. **Through rebellion.** Rebellion is oftentimes the result of anxiousness. We all want something, but Satan wants us to become anxious for whatever it is that we want. All too often, the thing that we want the most is marriage, and Satan uses this desire to advance against us romantically. But first, he has to get us to rebel against the Word of God. Satan often sends narcissists after prophetic individuals (empaths), and then he tries to get them into sin with the narcissist. Why is this important? Because Satan needs a sin offering to advance against any given state! So, the narcissist employs a tactic called "love bombing" where he or she says any and everything that we want to hear. But remember, this information will go and sit in the waiting rooms of our souls. The narcissist rushes us to send this information through and admit it into our hearts as truths; this way, the narcissist can secure his or her position in our lives by creating a soul tie. He or she then uses that soul tie to

filter in more lies, more promises, more threats, etc. Nevertheless, as horrible and as toxic as the narcissist is, he or she got in through the door or rebellion.

8. **Through covetousness.** Another word for "covetousness" is "jealousy." When jealousy enters a person's heart, it creates a window between the waiting room (conscious) and the heart (subconscious). This window creates what we call tunnel vision. It causes the individual bound by the spirit of jealousy to focus quite a bit of his or her energy and time on the person he or she is in competition with. And whatever has our attention also has our finances. The United States of America is a capitalistic nation because covetousness has been normalized so-much-so that it's rare to find someone who has embraced and accepted his or her own unique identity. Most people are trying to look, sound and live like their favorite celebrities. Consequently, Americans spend $10.7 billion on clothing each year! This doesn't count the $960 that the average American woman spends on her hair each year! When we factor in accessories, makeup and all of the items we invest in to enhance our appearances, Americans spend more than the national debt on decorating themselves each year! Don't get me wrong. There's nothing wrong with enhancing your beauty; the point I'm making is—most of our spending is the direct result of us competing with someone

else. This gives the enemy access to many Americans in the financial state.

And of course, these aren't the only windows that the enemy uses.

The state of a man will determine:

1. **The status of that man:** This is the condition that he's in.
2. **The stature of that man:** This is the maturity (or lack thereof) of a man.
3. **The statutes of a man:** These are the laws by which he governs himself.

Of course, the laws that come out of each state are determined by whomever it is that is sitting on the throne (beliefs) of that particular state. All the same, each state neighbors another state. For example, Satan often enters the parental state through rejection or neglect. He uses this as a springboard to access the romantic state of a person. He uses the romantic state to enter into the sexual state, and he'll keep advancing until he has taken over the mental state. So, if you've been dealing, for example, with the narcissist your whole life, you can't just break up with the person and think that you're free. Breaking up with the narcissist doesn't remove the bridge created by the trauma from that relationship or the trauma before that relationship. This is why most people find themselves dating the same demon in a different man or woman over and over again. What this means is—to break this stronghold or cycle of attracting and being attracted to toxic and broken people, you must first assess your status to determine what state (condition) you're in. After this, you have to address that particular state to get the information, the therapy and the deliverance you'll need to reclaim and fortify that area.

Please note that you can be a great person in one state and a broken, immature and manipulative person in another state. The same is true for others. This is why someone can be a friend of yours in one state, but an enemy of yours in another state. For example, your closest friend may be an amazing woman who's both loyal and integral as a friend, but in the financial state, she can outright be an enemy. This is because she lacks financial integrity, and wherever there is a lack of integrity, there is a lack of information or, better yet, a void. Because of this, she may be incredibly irresponsible as it relates to money, so loaning money to her could absolutely destroy your friendship. This is because, for one, she has a wrongful relationship with money, and two, she believes that everyone she's indebted to should consider her "situation" before asking her to return the money she's borrowed from them. In truth, she doesn't believe that she should have to repay anyone, even though she's promised to do so. Whenever she borrows money, she's friendly and humble, but whenever it's time to repay the money, she doesn't bother mentioning it. You have to literally ask for it back, and whenever you do, she immediately gets offended. "I'll give you every penny of your money back on tomorrow," she says scornfully. And the next day, she either doesn't call you or she'll talk about everything but the money she owes you. You have to "remind" her again, and when you do, she gets offended all over again. She will then send you the money via CashApp, Paypal or through some other method, and after that, she refuses to talk to you for a few days. Financially speaking, she's your enemy! This is because her financial state is in ruins. She even gets offended when her pastor starts talking about tithes and offerings. Remember, voids create a vacuum effect where they cause people to be attracted to one another in several states based on a need or several needs. So, she may be attracted to your financial state because it looks a lot better than hers, but unfortunately, you cannot connect with her in this area. The reason for this is:

1. **She needs to connect with a financial mentor (advisor), and not a financial friend.** What's the difference? Someone who wants to connect with you using the soul tie of friendship in a particular state is asking to defeat or remove the wall between your finances and their finances. This is both dangerous and foolish, especially when that person's financial state has been destroyed. Consequently, that person's ideologies and systems will begin to integrate themselves with your ideologies and systems, creating (in a sense) one purse between you and the person. This allows the enemy to use the soul tie between you and that person to cross over into your financial state, where he will then begin to act as a vacuum in your finances. However, a financial

advisor does not connect his or her finances with the person he or she is advising. This is because the advisor is not and will not create an intimate relationship with the person he or she is advising, but will instead, connect the person with the information he or she needs to rebuild his or her financial state.

2. **A friend in need is not a friend indeed.** While this quote is ambiguous, it is generally interpreted to mean that a true friend is there to give you his or her support whenever you are in need of it. And while this can be true in some instances, in many cases, it's not true. I dare to say this—a friend who knows when to support you and when to let you fall is a sister or brother indeed and in deed. Consider Israel as they journeyed through the wilderness into the Promised Land. To get them to keep moving, God had to ensure that there was no water in some areas for them to drink from. What this means is that whenever God wants us to move out of a mindset or He wants to evict us out of a comfort zone, He will oftentimes dry up the resources in that area. If a friend supplies you in your rebellion, rather than allowing God to provoke you to leave a mindset or a reality that is detrimental to you, that person is not a friend. Please note that an enemy is not a man or a woman who doesn't like you; an enemy is a person who gets between you and your God-given assignment, whether they do this while acknowledging themselves as enemies or they do this by masquerading themselves as friends. A true, God-

sent friend will let you become so financially frustrated until you finally get up and do something about it!

3. **She might be an enemy in disguise.** Remember, we discussed the nature of a void and its vacuum effect. Again, voids are like black holes in space; they have a strong gravitational pull. We call this pull attraction. Sometimes, people are financially attracted to you, but because they lack integrity, they'll try to connect with you in another state, and they'll use that state to slowly but surely migrate into your financial state. So, she may have used, for example, your love for sports or your love for fashion to connect with you, but in truth, she had been eyeing you from afar, admiring everything from the car you drive to your job description. From there, she said within her heart, "I'd love to be friends with that woman" or "I need friends like that in my life," and while this sounds harmless, the truth is, she used deception to gain access to your life. And wherever there's deception, there's a host of other issues that have to be resolved. You see, if she had asked you to mentor her, this would have been fine, but she chose to be a friend instead. Why is this wrong? People typically do this when they want the benefits of friendship, but not the responsibilities associated with mentorship, including having to pay for an advisor. In other words, they want a one-sided relationship with you, with them being the beneficiaries and you being the benefactor. This is because they want to create a soul tie between

themselves and you in a particular state, but they don't want the boundaries associated with mentorship or whatever label they qualify for. And you'll discover that these people are not your friends when you deny them access to the areas or resources that they are most interested in. For example, if a new friend of yours is constantly asking for advice about entrepreneurship, answer the friend once or twice, but after this, ask the person if he or she would like you to become his or her advisor, making note that there is a fee for mentorship. Chances are, the individual will say, "No, I just had a few questions." Answer the questions and change the subject. If he or she revisits the topic or asks for more help, tell the person that you'll draft up some packages that he or she could choose from for mentorship. Is this offensive? Absolutely! Because we often share this information freely with friends, and the individual is disguising himself or herself as a friend to get access to this information. So yes, he or she will be offended, and that's okay! Friendship is balanced; there's some give and some take, but whenever there's more take than give, you are not entertaining a friend, you are entertaining someone who's set their heart on taking advantage of you. Contracts and fees will always chase people like this away. And please note, you have to be willing to offend people; this doesn't mean that you have to be rude or offensive, it simply means that you should have boundaries in every state, and you shouldn't give people access to information that they haven't earned (for lack of a better term).

The point is—you have to examine the status (condition) and stature (maturity) of a person to determine if he or she can connect with you in certain areas and how that person should connect with you in certain areas. A millionaire would not financially connect himself or herself with someone who's in poverty, because regardless of popular beliefs, being a millionaire versus being broke is not a money issue; it's an information issue. It has everything to do with how each individual thinks, and of course, how a person thinks is largely rooted in:

1. That person's experiences.
2. That person's knowledge or lack thereof.
3. That person's understanding (interpretation) of that knowledge.
4. That person's environment; these are the people he or she surrounds himself or herself with and the information that he or she feeds himself or herself regularly (books, television, music).
5. That person's beliefs.

Why is all of this important? If you've had problems setting or enforcing boundaries, you've had quite a few broken, toxic and narcissistic people to come into your life, overstay their welcome and rob you of everything that was valuable to you, including your peace. It's important for you to get a more in-depth look at yourself to better understand why you've gone through what you've gone through and how to prevent those problems from reoccurring in the future. All the same, you have to examine your own status and stature in each of these states; this will allow you to specifically target those areas where you lack information and those areas that have been impacted by trauma. As a teacher, coach and mentor, I've found that the large majority of people who've complained about narcissists or being taken advantage of had no true clue as to who they were in Christ; they had no true knowledge of themselves. Consequently, they kept introducing people to who they wanted to be or who they thought they were, only to find themselves being broken and rejected all the more. They didn't know their makeups; most of them didn't know that they were prophetic or how Satan attacks prophetic people. So, they went about life, casually meeting people and repeatedly getting hurt, wondering if there was something wrong with them. The problem is this—the Jezebel spirit which again is the spirit behind narcissism is passionately after prophets and prophetic people! Let's look at that spirit's history.

The Jezebel Spirit

1 Kings 18:3-4: And Ahab called Obadiah, which was the governor of his house. (Now Obadiah feared the LORD greatly: For it was so, when Jezebel cut off the prophets of the LORD, that Obadiah took an hundred prophets, and hid them by fifty in a cave, and fed them with bread and water.)

Revelation 2:20: But I have this against you, that you

tolerate that woman Jezebel, who calls herself a prophetess and is teaching and seducing my servants to practice sexual immorality and to eat food sacrificed to idols.

Please note that this was the first mention of that spirit's agenda, but that spirit had been around for thousands of years. It acquired the name the Jezebel spirit when the Apostle John, thousands of years after Jezebel's reign and death, released the prophetic words listed in Revelation 2:20. God wasn't talking about the woman Jezebel since she was dead; He was talking about:

1. A demonic spirit.
2. A demonic system.

It was referred to as a woman because that spirit often manifests itself in and through women. Yes, it does enter and manifest itself through men as well, but it prefers women, especially in a spiritual setting. (Interesting fact: when referencing this spirit in women, people tend to use the term "Jezebel spirit" but when referencing this spirit in men, people tend to use the term "narcissist"). And please note that while it was Satan himself who tempted Eve in the Garden of Eden, what was birthed through her disobedience was a demonic system. Eve not only disobeyed God, but she also tempted her husband into sin, and it was for this reason that God gave Adam (man) the seat of authority over Eve (woman). In Genesis 3:16, God spoke to Eve. "Unto the woman he said, I will greatly multiply thy sorrow and thy conception; in sorrow thou shalt bring forth children; and thy

desire shall be to thy husband, and he shall rule over thee."
Just in case you aren't an avid Bible reader, please note that
God did render judgment to Satan and to the man, Adam.
Nevertheless, when He told Eve that her husband would rule
over her, He was dealing with a system that had been
birthed through her disobedience. God clearly saw the
system that Satan was trying to create; this was a system
he'd tried to create in Heaven when he'd deceived one-third
of God's angels. He'd attempted to use the weaker vessels
which, of course, were the angels to override God's
hierarchical system. He wanted to be like God, which means
that he wanted to be on the same plane, at minimum, as
God. To accomplish his wicked agenda, Satan (called Lucifer
at that time), lied to the angels made them think that God
was withholding something good from them. He then went
on to tell them that they could be independent of God; they
could be equal to God. This was all a lie! And of course, it
caused a great divide between the angels, and
consequently, there was war in Heaven; this war was
mentioned in Revelation 12:7. Satan and his angels lost the
war and were cast out of Heaven and into the Earth. And
one day, Satan spotted Eve in the Garden of Eden, so he
possessed the body of a snake and made his way over to
her, where he proceeded to deceive her into rebelling
against God. Eve was the weaker vessel because God
created Adam from the dust of the ground, and He breathed
life into his nostrils, but He'd pulled Eve out of Adam. This
means that she was the second born, and let's remember
why God created Eve. He said in Genesis 2:18 that it is not

good for man to be alone. He created Eve to accompany Adam; He also created her to help him with his assignment. This may sound offensive to the modern-day woman because of all the feminist movements but, in truth, God designed it this way to protect the woman since she was and is the weaker vessel. Sure, we're strong in many ways, but emotionally speaking, women are weaker because—get this—we're wired to feel! What does this mean? We are help meets. One of the strengths that a wife has is the ability to sense when something is wrong with her husband; this provokes her to strategically pray for her husband and her household. It also helps her to set the atmosphere in their home. This is why, traditionally speaking, women were homemakers; we picked out the furniture and decided where it would be placed. Women are atmosphere setters; we are designed to be prophetic! This is what it means to be the weaker vessel! After all, we have to remember that He created us, so try as we may, we don't have the right, the authority and we shouldn't have the audacity to tell Him how to be God. Remember, Satan didn't approach Adam; instead, he decided to approach and deceive Eve. God would go on to employ systems to protect women from being misled by Satan; for example, in the Old Testament, a man could not go directly to a woman and ask her out on a date. Again, this was because of her sensitivity level. He had to go through her father to get to her, and he had to marry the woman; there was no dating back then. He had to watch her from afar and look at the integrity of her family to decide if he wanted to partner with that family through marriage. And of course, someone would say, "Well, what if they weren't compatible?" The answer is—compatibility, regardless of what we've come to believe, is a sin issue. If the man loved God and was following Jewish tradition, and the same was true for the woman, there was nothing that he could possibly want that would conflict with what his wife wanted. Think about it. Compatibility is an issue today because of the normalization of sin. For example, a believing man can easily say that a believing woman is not compatible with him, and he may be telling the truth because the woman in question hasn't matured yet. She may still be looking for something to quench her many voids, and because of this, she's always hanging around a bunch of double-minded busy bodies who are both religious and prideful. The man, on the other hand, may be looking for a woman who loves the Lord with all of her heart and strength; he's looking for someone who is content and ready to walk alongside him on their journey. At the same time, the issue could be the man himself! Maybe he's double-minded, lustful, prideful and entitled, and the woman in question is way too sold out to the Lord for him. Amos 3:3 says, "Can two walk together except they be agreed?" In short, these people have not agreed on the basics, which is how to serve God.

Again, Jezebel is both a spirit and a system. This system is designed to destroy the voice of God by destroying the prophets of God. Prophets and prophetic people echo God's voice in the Earth. Also, be reminded that the Jezebel spirit has been around since before the birth of Jezebel. It is the same spirit that came after Israel time and time again, for example, it is the same spirit that:

1. **Tempted Cain to kill Abel.** Both of these sons represented systems; one was a system of worship. The other was a system of works. The system of works attempted to muzzle and destroy the system of worship. In other words, religion tried to silence relationship. Note: the Jezebel spirit is a religious spirit. This does not mean that every person who has this spirit is religious; it simply means that they have patterns designed to bring about a certain result. For example, a Jezebellic man may punish his God-fearing, church-going wife by refusing to go to church with her and leaving the house every time she goes to church. He will often send her a text while she's in church saying, "I'll be watching the game with a few of my friends. See you later!" When she arrives home, he'll refuse to respond to her text messages or answer her phone calls. He may even turn his phone off! The goal is to punish her until she finally stops going to church. This is something he does religiously.

2. **Provoked Ham to expose his father, Noah.** People with the Jezebel spirit (narcissists) almost always threaten to expose the people they are trying to control. They do this to gain leverage and remain in control. Recognizing the system that Satan was attempting to rebirth in the Earth through Ham, Noah cursed Ham's seed, Canaan, which was his second son. Please note that Noah wasn't (per se) speaking a

curse or wishing a curse over Canaan, he prophetically identified and acknowledged a generational curse that would travel through Ham's son, Canaan.

3. **Incited Joseph's brothers to sell him into slavery.**
   Satan recognized where the mantle of Jacob (Israel) would fall, so he provoked jealousy in Joseph's brothers. You see, Satan knew that Jesus was going to come into the Earth through the womb of a woman, so he worked diligently to monitor God's movements through His prophets. And when he saw the favor of God on Israel (also known as Jacob), he began to monitor Israel's sons. The minute he recognized that Israel favored Joseph over all his sons, he set out to destroy Joseph.

Other appearances of the Jezebel spirit in history include:
1. Pharaoh enslaving God's people in Egypt.
2. When Miriam and Aaron got together to gossip about Moses.
3. The oppression of Israel by the Philistines, and the use of Delilah to get Samson to reveal the secrets of his superhuman strength.
4. The moment Saul disobeyed God. This is called usurping authority.
5. The moment Saul began his campaign to kill David, God's chosen.
6. The attempt of Absalom, David's son, to turn the hearts of the people away from his father, the king of

Israel. And the attempt of Absalom to kill his father to usurp his authority.

7. Haman's plots and plans to kill off all of the Jews that resided in Persia simply because they would not bow down to him.

8. The attempt of King Herod to locate Jesus when he was a baby so that he could kill him.

9. Herodias asking for the head of John, the Baptist, on a platter.

10. The repeated beatings and imprisonment of the apostles.

There are countless mentions of this spirit throughout the Bible, and it's objective has always been the same—to silence the voice of the prophets and to stop or delay the movements of God in the Earth. And of course, it's not just after prophets and prophetic people, it passionately detests apostles and apostolic people. The goal of this spirit is to stop the Word of God from coming to pass or to, at minimum, cause as many delays as humanly and spiritually possible. And this is why he targets women because we represent the birthing systems of God.

Revelation 12:13-17: And when the dragon saw that he was cast unto the earth, he persecuted the woman which brought forth the man child. And to the woman were given two wings of a great eagle, that she might fly into the wilderness, into her place, where she is nourished for a time, and times, and half a time, from the face of the serpent. And the serpent cast out of his mouth water as a flood after the woman, that he might cause her to be carried away of the flood. And the earth helped the woman, and the earth opened her mouth, and swallowed up the flood which the dragon cast out of his mouth. And the dragon was wroth with the woman, and went to make war with the remnant of her seed, which keep the commandments of God, and have the testimony of Jesus Christ.

Now, try this. Reread the scripture above and replace the word "woman" with "prophet," and you'll better understand why Satan is passionately after your voice and your ministerial assignment.

The Ahab'ed Empath

Every empath is not an Ahab, but every Ahab is an empath. And by Ahab, I'm dealing with individuals who have been bound by the Ahab spirit; this spirit is a hybrid of fear, rejection, rebellion, ambition and religiousness. People bound by this spirit tend to exhibit many of the following characteristics:

1. Fear of authority.
2. Fear of confrontation.
3. Idolatrous tendencies. They will often say things like, "I love hard," which often means that they tend to obsess over and overly commit themselves to people whenever they get romantically involved with someone.

4. Little to no boundaries.
5. Little to no true fear of God.
6. A tendency to be attracted to and/or attract controlling, manipulative and religious or rebellious people.
7. Co-dependency.
8. Addictive behaviors.
9. A tendency to relinquish control over what's important or valuable to them in exchange for love, acceptance or affirmation.
10. An almost insatiable need to fit in or be accepted.

Of course, this is just a short list of characteristics. But what would cause a person to embrace such a wicked and castrating spirit? All too often, the individual had his or her voice stolen at a young age; this is oftentimes the result of a toxic or emotionally unhealthy parent constantly silencing the child and not trusting a lot of what the child had to say. This causes the child to question himself or herself, and when children who've been repeatedly silenced become adults, they simply do not feel they have anything valuable to say. This causes them to become relatively insecure, passive and fearful. This insecurity often causes them to admire people who appear to be bold, confident and even confrontational, and all too often, they confuse rudeness with boldness. For example, a timid young man moved into a new neighborhood with his mother and was immediately targeted by a few of the local bullies; we'll call him Arnold. Arnold found himself too scared to go outside because one of his bullies lived directly next door to his mother's house; we'll call this bully Jason. One day, Arnold went outside to check the mail, and to his surprise, he saw his bully being bullied by another young boy named Patrick. "Pick on someone who's not afraid of you!" shouted Patrick as he stood over Jason. Arnold was impressed; Patrick was doing something that he didn't have the courage to do. A few days later, Arnold spotted Patrick again, but this time, the boys were at the mall. "What are you looking at?!" Patrick shouted at a young man twice his size who happened to be staring menacingly at him. Two weeks later, Arnold walked into his new classroom. He was now a senior in high school and school had just started for the year. And to his surprise, he spotted Patrick again. As it turned out, he was also a senior in high school. Later that day, Patrick became frustrated with their new teacher, Mr. Ronald; this was because Mr. Ronald had spent the last thirty minutes trying to assert his dominance over the class. He'd assigned seats to everyone, forcing the students to get out of the seats they'd chosen for themselves and sit wherever Mr. Ronald told them to sit. To make matters worse, he'd tried to intimidate a few of the young boys who'd displayed any form of disdain towards his new seating arrangements. He'd gotten in their faces and raised his voice at them. This charade ended when he'd attempted to intimidate Patrick. Instead of lowering his head and sitting down like the rest of the young men had done, Patrick stood in place and stared Mr. Waldron in his eyes without blinking. His face was stern and his body was relaxed. This stare-down lasted for two minutes before Mr.

Ronald finally walked away. "Sit down," he'd said to Patrick as he retreated to his seat. "You're not as tough as you think you are." Nevertheless, Arnold was impressed. To him, Patrick appeared to be fearless, bold, confident and cool. So, when Patrick found himself looking for his pen one day in class, Arnold happily handed him one of his pens. This behavior would continue on for several months. Arnold would always provide Patrick with school supplies whenever he was low, and he'd even helped him with his homework a few times. After this, the two young men became friends, but their friendship wasn't centered around a common interest; it was centered around Arnold's fears and Patrick's needs. This was the birth of an Ahab/Jezebel or, better yet, empath/narcissist relationship. This is similar to the biblical figure, Ahab, and the illegal alliance he'd formed with Phoenicia. This was strictly a political move. Terrified of the other nations that had been emerging as some of the most prolific and powerful nations in Asia, Ahab decided to disobey God by partnering with a pagan nation. And to solidify his treaty with Phoenicia, Ahab married the king of Phoenicia's daughter, Jezebel. He then gave her the highest seat or office that a woman could hold, and that is the role of queen. Now, it goes without saying that most people would naturally assume that because Ahab was king over Israel, there was no other role that his new bride, Jezebel, could serve in other than the role of queen, but this is not true. It was customary in that time for kings to have multiple wives and countless concubines, however, only one woman would be crowned queen. Consider this fact—Ahab had seventy sons at the time of his death. And we don't know how many daughters he had; we do, however, know that he'd fathered Athaliah, a wicked woman who would eventually kill off almost every male who could potentially stake claim to the throne of Judah. So, we can safely guess that Ahab had over one hundred children. Studies show that a woman can have around 15 pregnancies in her lifetime, which means that she could give birth to anywhere between 15-30 children. One woman broke that record; her name was Feodor Vassilyev and she was born in 1707. Mrs. Vassilyev gave birth to 69 children after 27 pregnancies, including 16 pairs of twins. The point is—Jezebel did not and could not have given birth to one hundred children. This means that Ahab had other wives and concubines, even though he'd crowned Jezebel as queen. And again, his decision to make her queen was centered around an alliance he'd formed between Israel and Phoenicia; this was because Ahab feared Phoenicia and he feared the other nations. In other words, he was the fearful young man who'd partnered with a bully in his attempt to shield himself from other bullies. And whenever this happens, the passive, fearful and insecure personality has to submit himself or herself to the dominant, fearless and confident personality. In exchange, the bully makes the bullied feel safe, wanted, appreciated and more confident.

Ahab'ed empaths tend to seek refuge in relationships (platonic, familial, romantic or spiritual), hoping that the people they connect themselves with will help them to feel more confident or, at minimum, those people will undertake the tasks that they consider to be scary or taxing. In exchange for this security, they tend to relinquish what's left of their voices and their identities. This is how they find themselves in relationships with the narcissistic personality, after all, the Jezebel spirit is attracted to authority that has not yet been tapped into. It is attracted to fear, loneliness, desperation, hopelessness, perversion, ambition and religion. It is, however, repelled by contentment and holiness. Think of it this way—a child drops a lollipop next to her father's car and leaves it there. This happens in mid-Spring. Thirty minutes later, her father comes outside and finds an army of ants near his rear tire. After investigating, he sees what the ants are feeding on. The ants, while pests, didn't randomly make their way into his driveway just to put on a show. They came because there was something on the ground that they were attracted to. This is how the Jezebel spirit (narcissist) tends to find its way to many prophetic people. It finds people who have pretty much laid down their authority in exchange for:

1. Security (financial or relational)
2. Love
3. Normality
4. Peace
5. A sense of belonging

It gives these people what they're looking for or, at minimum, a generic form of what they're looking for, in exchange for the authority they chose to relinquish. This simply means that in order for us to finally rid ourselves of the narcissistic personalities who have invaded our lives, we have to be willing to:

1. Take accountability for our wrongs.
2. Take responsibility for ourselves. In other words, stop relying on people to do for us what God has given us the ability to do for ourselves!

We can do this by:

1. **Changing our status.** In other words, we have to change the status of our hearts by addressing every state that makes up our souls, and we must get healed, delivered and educated in all of those states. This takes time and consistency, but it's well worth the investment!
2. **Changing our stature.** We do this by getting the education and information we'll need to grow out of one season and into the next. This simply means that we make it a point to chase knowledge, embrace understanding and accept wisdom.
3. **Building and securing our statutes.** These are our standards and the laws by which we govern ourselves. First and foremost, we must have standards; we can't haphazardly allow ourselves to be led by our emotions. And next, we must respect and enforce our standards, regardless of who we offend and repel from our lives.

In summary, we defeat the Jezebel spirit by defeating fear! Jezebel smells fear and comes to feed on it. This means that we can't rid ourselves of the narcissistic personality until we learn to walk in the authority God has granted to us. When this happens, the Ahab spirit loses its grounds, and consequently, Jezebel loses its crown. Remember this—in the realm of the spirit, Jezebel is married to Ahab, so if you don't want to deal with the narcissist, cast out and reject the Ahab spirit.

THE BURDEN OF BOUNDARIES

"And Ahab the son of Omri did evil in the sight of the LORD above all that were before him.
And it came to pass, as if it had been a light thing for him to walk in the sins of Jeroboam the son of Nebat, that he took to wife Jezebel the daughter of Ethbaal king of the Zidonians, and went and served Baal, and worshiped him" (1 Kings 16:30-31).

"We're almost home! That's one of the altars of our God up ahead, and in the distance, you can see the Holy Temple!" Ahab was excited about showing his new bride the place he'd grown up. She'd never been to Israel before, and he wanted her to love the place. After excitedly speaking to his new bride, Ahab sped past his wife on his prized camel. He wanted to impress her, after all, her father was big news to him. Jezebel smiled at her new husband before looking in the direction of the Holy Temple. The wind blew through her long, dark hair, revealing her oddly arranged features. "I hate this place," she thought to herself, mentally mapping out all of the changes that she would be making—effective immediately. Twenty minutes later, Jezebel's camel came to the Israeli boundary and lifted its hoof. All of Heaven and Earth seemed to stand still as the camel brought the very embodiment of Satan across the border. Finally, Jezebel leaped from her camel at the dismay of her maidservants.

"I'm okay!" she said, dusting off her queenly apparel. She left out a sigh of disbelief as her beautifully crafted sandals filled with sand. "Oh lord, help me," she mumbled under her breath, but of course, she wasn't talking to our Lord and Savior. She was speaking of and to the god she worshiped—she was speaking to a deaf deity by the name of Baal.

But this hadn't been the first boundary that Ahab had violated with Jezebel, and it definitely wouldn't be the last. Just days prior to this event, the couple had exchanged vows in an elaborate ceremony at her father's castle back in Phoenicia. So, his first violation had been him making a deal with a pagan king, and next, marrying that king's daughter in an attempt to create an alliance between Israel and Phoenicia.

And while the aforementioned story is probably an overly exaggerated account of the newlywed's first entrance into Samaria (in Northern Israel) as a couple, the fact does remain that:

1. Ahab, like his father, violated the commandments of God by causing Israel to sin. In other words, he instituted or allowed the worship of other deities.
2. Ahab's father, Omri, made peace with the local Canaanites and accepted their religion in an attempt to reduce tension between the Israelites and the Canaanites. In other words, he accepted their gods, rather than sticking by his own.
3. Omri may have arranged the marriage between

Jezebel and his son, Ahab, nevertheless, Ahab followed through with the marriage, even though it was against Jewish tradition, and more importantly, against God's commands.

4. Ahab brought Jezebel into Samaria where he'd created a temple for Baal, the deity she worshiped.
5. Ahab allowed Jezebel to make Baal worship the official religion and to kill off anyone who would not submit to her god, including many of God's prophets.

These are the facts. God had specifically told Israel not to intermarry with other faiths in Deuteronomy 7:1-6, which reads, "When the LORD thy God shall bring thee into the land whither thou goest to possess it, and hath cast out many nations before thee, the Hittites, and the Girgashites, and the Amorites, and the Canaanites, and the Perizzites, and the Hivites, and the Jebusites, seven nations greater and mightier than thou; and when the LORD thy God shall deliver them before thee; thou shalt smite them, and utterly destroy them; thou shalt make no covenant with them, nor shew mercy unto them: Neither shalt thou make marriages with them; thy daughter thou shalt not give unto his son, nor his daughter shalt thou take unto thy son. For they will turn away thy son from following me, that they may serve other gods: so will the anger of the LORD be kindled against you, and destroy thee suddenly. But thus shall ye deal with them; ye shall destroy their altars, and break down their images, and cut down their groves, and burn their graven images with fire. For thou art an holy people unto the LORD thy God:

the LORD thy God hath chosen thee to be a special people unto himself, above all people that are upon the face of the earth."

Nevertheless, Ahab crossed the point of no return; he did exactly what God said he would do if he intermarried with another nation. What's interesting is, throughout the scriptures, God would often say that the people sinned to provoke Him to wrath. Like many of you, I didn't fully understand what He meant for several years. Why would someone want to *intentionally* provoke God? Who would be that foolish and what did they hope to accomplish by doing so? Here's what I learned just from observing modern-day believers. We all want something. Every single one of us has something in view or, if we want to be technical, we have several objectives or destinations in our sights. Whether that goal is marriage, parenthood, wealth, revenge or peace, we all have a mental map that we rarely acknowledge. On this map, there are several small points, all of which represent places and seasons, along with one major destination. We've invested time, energy, blood, sweat, tears and resources into our journeys toward our personal promised lands. God told us to seek the Kingdom of God first and all of His righteousness; He said that by doing so, He would give us everything else (see Matthew 6:33). This scripture denotes protocol. You see, there's something about the human psychology that God knows that most believers have yet to discover, and that is, whatever we seek first becomes a god to us. So, God is pretty much telling us to put Him and

174

His Kingdom on the forefront of our minds; this way, He can give us His heart. When we have His heart, we'll do His will, but if not, we'll create a mental map of goals, objectives and destinations that we want to venture into, and this isn't entirely bad, however, it becomes bad when it's not done in order. This is because those places suddenly become big to us, meaning, they become like gods. This is why so many women are obsessed marriage; they don't necessarily understand what marriage is, but they are in love with the idea of what marriage appears to be. This is also why divorce statistics are at an all-time high.

When something becomes big to us, it becomes a god to us. Please understand that it is possible for a person to intentionally or unintentionally worship other gods. Jezebel worshiped many deities, but she considered Baal to be her supreme god. Believers still do this today. Many Christians have acknowledged Jesus Christ as their Lord and Savior, HOWEVER, if He were to print off the maps that He sees in their hearts, He'd show them that they have other gods who they've esteemed over Him. Whether those gods are marriage, money or fame, it became bigger than the Most High God to them, so they pursued their deities of choice, and Christianity was nothing more than a small stop-off point on their personal maps. Anytime we place anything before YAHWEH, we set ourselves up to fail, after all, we need God to prosper in any and everything! There isn't a single thing that you can do without God! So, what I've witnessed over the years is believers chasing marriage, money and influence (just to name a few). At some point, many of them began to experience the gods that they had been chasing. This only increased their appetites for those informal deities. Before long, they were "in love" with a person, a lifestyle, an idea or a position (just to name a few). But one day, the very thing that they idolized began to slip away from them, and they panicked. They tried everything to hold onto their gods, but to no avail. They then called on the name of the Lord, hoping He'd intervene, but why would the Most High God help a person to stay in idolatry? Why would He answer such a prayer favorably? James 4:3 confirms this; it reads, "Ye ask, and receive not, because ye ask amiss, that ye may consume it upon your lusts."

When it rains, it pours—or at least, that's what "they" say. The woman has lost the very thing that she'd made a god of—her lover. And to add insult to injury, her job suddenly lays her off. And finally, she receives the news that one of her uncles is on his death bed. "I've been going to church faithfully," the heartbroken believer says. "I've tithed, fasted and prayed fervently, but God still let that man hurt me the way that he did. And He just keeps on letting the devil attack me. So, what am I serving Him for? It's clear to me that He doesn't care anything about me or what I'm going through." Anger begins to fill the heart of the believer, but it's not necessarily an anger that is verbally expressed. Instead, it begins to manifest in the believer's choices. "That's okay," says the jilted lover in her heart. "When you try to do right, wrong happens to you, so from now on, I'll treat men the way they've treated me." So, the scorned Christian goes and intentionally sins against God. She starts hanging with the wrong crowd, going to clubs, fornicating and drinking excessively. Nevertheless, she continues to come to church (whenever she feels like it) and she continues to refer to herself a Christian. However, she's taken another position. She now loathes Christians who have taken the holiness approach; she adores the double-minded believers who ally themselves with her anger by saying things like, "It doesn't take all that," referencing the choices of believers who intentionally try to make the right choices. What she's doing is called "provoking God to wrath." In short, she's trying to force God to respond to her, after all, it would appear that He hadn't answered her prayers whenever her now estranged lover was in the process of breaking her heart. It would appear that He hadn't answered her when her job security was in danger, and it would appear that He hadn't answered her when her uncle was on the brink of death. Angry and determined to provoke God, she went on a sinning-spree, doing just about everything she knew to be wrong. And for several years, God does not respond to her. He allows her to flaunt her sin, even in the church; that is, until one day, the very sin that she's come to love begins to request its wages. This is what it means to provoke God to wrath.

Ahab's father, Omri, was obviously angry with YAHWEH. People who get angry with God often do so when they have a misunderstanding of who He is. What they do is humanize Him and attempt to have a transactional relationship with

Him, whereas, they serve Him in exchange for His "yes" and "amen." But here's the thing—they are trying to get God to serve them, but they don't realize this. And God, the Creator, is not about to serve something He created! Nevertheless, they continue in sin, hoping that one of God's prophets will corner them and tell them how desperate God is for them to return to Him. This way, they can begin bargaining with God. Again, this is a transactional mindset and it is very common in today's church. But the prophet passes them on by and prays for someone else. When the prophet does make his or her way to them, God doesn't address their anger; instead, He speaks of the assignment on their lives. They leave church confused. Why is God still talking about using them, and why hasn't He answered their other petitions? The answer is simple—God's not about to explain Himself to flesh! His ways are above our ways and His thoughts above our thoughts (see Isaiah 55:8).

Ahab brought his new bride over the border, and behind her came a network of devils, with Death standing in the rear. Many prophets would lose their lives because Ahab gave a narcissist authority over them. Many Israelites would find themselves in groves worshiping Asherah and Baal, in their attempts to stay alive. They'd have to listen to sermons about these devilish deities and sing songs of praise to these strange gods.

Ahab had a responsibility to the people of Israel, after all, the word Israel (Yisra'el) was taken from the Hebrew name which means "God contends." Israel, of course, was named after Jacob, a Hebrew patriarch who'd once wrestled with God. As the king of northern Israel, Ahab didn't just have a responsibility, he had a great responsibility, meaning, because he was on a platform, his sins would also be platformed. Any sin that he struggled with as the head of Israel would affect the members. "But he that knew not, and did commit things worthy of stripes, shall be beaten with few stripes. For unto whomsoever much is given, of him shall be much required: and to whom men have committed much, of him they will ask the more" (Luke 12:48).

We all have a measure of responsibility, and depending on the assignments that God has given us, those responsibilities range from small to great. Some people don't have much a responsibility because they haven't been "given much." This doesn't mean that God doesn't love them; it simply means that He took their strengths and weaknesses into account before they were even born. He knew what their grandparents struggled with. He knew what their parents struggled with. And He also knew what they would struggle with. So, He gave them the measure of responsibility that they could bear, and then, to others, He gave a greater amount of responsibility. This is why for some of us, we can't get away with the sins others so freely indulge in. So, while other believers enjoy their free roam all over the land of sin, jumping between the church and the world and flaunting their sins for others to see, many of us have the beautiful (and heavy) burden of God's trust. And while having God's trust is a blessing, it can oftentimes feel like a burden because one wrong choice on our ends can end in public shame. I joked with a woman once about sexual immorality, and I said to her that because of the platform God has given me, I have to make sure I stay far away from it. I don't desire it anymore (thank God), and I am cognizant of the burden I bear. If I sin, I cause others to fall with me. I joked with the woman that if I were to "mess around" one time for even a few seconds, I'd likely end up pregnant and I'd look like I was six months pregnant whenever I was three months pregnant. And while we laughed at the notion, I was simply acknowledging the burden that I carried. And please understand that when I say burden, I'm not saying that it's something I don't want to carry; I am privileged, grateful and blessed to have God's trust, however, when I say burden, I'm talking about the tight boundaries that God has drawn around me—boundaries that I've learned to love and respect.

Of course, your question may be, "Why do God seem to bless, protect and keep some people when they are in sin, but for others, He doesn't extend the same measure of grace?" The answer is twofold.

1. Romans 5:20: Moreover the law entered, that the offence might abound. But where sin abounded, grace did much more abound.
2. The second answer is favor. Who of the two people would you say God has extended the most favor to—the person who is in flagrant discord with the

Bible or the ones who can't seem to get away with anything? The second one, of course! The sin-loving Christian gets grace, but the faithful Christian gets favor! But one of the attributes of favor is correction. "For whom the LORD loveth he correcteth; even as a father the son in whom he delighteth" (Proverbs 3:12).

It is important to note that every believer has God-instituted boundaries around them. Every believer is supposed to uphold, respect and enforce those boundaries. All the same, every believer has the same Bible, meaning, what's a sin for me is also a sin for you. The only difference is, one believer has God's trust, and with His trust, comes a greater measure of responsibility. With the greater responsibility comes a greater reward and/or a greater punishment. By punishment, I'm not talking about fire and brimstone; I'm talking about the burden of disappointing the Most High God or, at minimum, feeling like you've disappointed Him.

"We're almost to my house!" The voice came from the driver's seat of a Corolla. But this time, Jezebel isn't in the passenger's seat. It was a modern-day believer by the name of Mia. Mia looked at all the well-kept homes in the area, noticing that they all were cookie-cutter, but they still looked nice. The Corolla pulled into a long driveway before making a complete stop. "This is it," said James as he turned to look at his uneasy girlfriend. The couple had met at church and they'd just finished going out on their fourth date, but after eating heartily, James had insisted that the couple stop by his house. He wanted to show her where he lived, and he wanted to change his clothes. The two of them had dined at a four-star restaurant, so he'd worn a pair of dress shoes to compliment his white shirt and gray slacks. After spending a couple of hours together, the couple decided that they weren't ready to go home just yet. Instead, they wanted to go for a walk on a beach nearby. "Come in," said James. "Don't worry. I won't bite. I just want to change my clothes right quick and I'd love to give you a tour of the house!" Mia looked at the beautiful two-story home. "This isn't a good idea," she thought to herself before exiting the car. Her heels rested on the pavement of the driveway, and almost immediately, a mosquito bit her on the ankle. She slapped her ankle repeatedly before following her new beau into his house.

In the house, Mia noticed how spacious, but empty the house was, minus a couple of old couches, a love seat and a poorly placed television. "Where's your bathroom?" she asked, looking into the dining room and noticing a folding table in place of what should have been a dining room table. "Use the one upstairs," James interrupted. "The one downstairs is out of order." Ironically enough, they were both out of order, but neither of them would be willing to admit this. Mia made her way up the steps with James just a few feet behind her. "This way," James said, pointing to an open door on the left side of the hall. Mia made her way into the bathroom, but before she could close the door, James rushed in. "Sorry," he said, hurriedly flushing the toilet. It was clear that he'd urinated a time or two, but he'd neglected to flush the toilet. "When you live alone, you don't think about this kinda stuff," James said jokingly as he exited the bathroom. Mia reached for the toilet paper. It was obviously cheap because it ripped the minute she tried to pull it. She used the small sheet to wipe the urine sprinkles off the seat before using the bathroom. After she was done using the bathroom, she made her way to the mirror. The sink hadn't been cleaned in a while. It was covered in shaved hairs that had clearly come from James' beard, plus, there was dried up toothpaste, and some odd blue substance in the sink. She looked in the mirror at herself, almost not recognizing the woman looking back at her. This is because she was in the midst of a perspective shift; at home earlier that day, she'd seen a queen looking back at her, but now, the enemy was messing with her mind. She looked soulless. Mia washed her hands and made her way out of the bathroom.

"Mia!" James laughed. Mia turned to the left, trying to trace James' voice. "What happened? Where are you?" she asked. "Here!" said James, inviting her into his bedroom. Mia stood in the doorway and leaned against the doorpost. She'd already crossed a few boundaries, but she knew that should she enter that bedroom, her three years of abstinence would become nothing but a distant memory. "Come in!" James said jokingly while looking at an old photo album. "I'm not gonna bite you! It's okay. I just want to show you something." Mia made her way into the bedroom, ignoring every intelligible voice of reason that dared to silently challenge her. "This is a picture of me when I was four. My mother said that I'd walked up to this cop; I don't know him by the way, and I'd pulled out a toy gun. She said that I told the cop to 'stick-em up.'" James laughed hysterically. I thank God that the man had a sense of humor. My Mom said that she was so humiliated that she offered to pay for the cop's cup of coffee. She said that man laughed it off and declined her offer, but she could tell that he wished he could do so much more. After that incident, she sent me to live with my father and his wife, and that's how I ended up in church. They were so afraid that I'd end up in prison or worse that they baptized me against my will at the age of four. Here's the picture of my baptism. As you can see, I was not happy." Mia laughed. "Wow. You were a terrible child. It's no wonder ..." Before Mia could finish her sentence, James suddenly leaned in and kissed her. At first, Mia pushed him away. "James, what are you doing? We can't do this..." But James didn't listen. He leaned in again and began to kiss her. This time, the kiss lasted for five seconds before Mia interrupted. "James, I ...." James moved in for another kiss; this time, lifting his body just above hers. "There's nothing wrong with kissing," Mia reasoned with herself internally. "We'll just kiss. Nothing more, nothing less." But that's not all they did that night. With every boundary crossed, Mia found herself even more tempted until they'd gone "all the way." Feeling guilty and ashamed, Mia excused herself to the bathroom while James lay on the bed fast asleep. She looked in the mirror and the almost lifeless woman she'd seen earlier looked right back at her. "You're not a real Christian! You're a whore! God is mad at you now!" Mia's thoughts began to overwhelm her. "Are you okay in there?" James voice shattered the sounds of the silent war she was in. "Yeah, I'm okay," Mia responded, turning off the light. Her breath tasted like his breath; her clothes smelled like a mixture of his cologne and his sweat. The curls that once framed her face were now flat. And her lipstick was pretty much gone, minus the little lipstick that had managed to survive James aggressive, but passionate kisses. When she turned around, she saw James standing in the doorway. He was wearing more of her lipstick than she was. "You ready?" he asked, his voice now sounding disinterested. "Yeah," said Mia, looking into her boyfriend's eyes and trying to read his mind. "Are you okay?" she asked. James grabbed his keys and let out a yawn. "Yeah," he said. "Just tired. Why don't I take you home and we can go walking on the beach tomorrow night?"

James and Mia's relationship continued for two years before they broke up due to his infidelities. What happened here is a common Christian lust story. Again, we all have the same boundaries, but Mia kept allowing hers to be violated; that is, until she found herself becoming nothing more than a stand-in wife. The same was true for James. When he took Mia to his house, he had a plan. And he'd turned off every voice of reason that dared to challenge his plans. So, how should Mia have handled this situation?

1. She should have refused to go to his house. Every Christian has to have boundaries or laws that they've personally set in place to help them navigate through

temptation. Countries don't prepare for war in times of war, they prepare for war in times of peace; this way, they can be well-equipped to fight off the advances of their enemies.

2. If he'd insisted and kept driving to his house, Mia should have called someone to pick her up or, at minimum, refused to get out of the car.

3. Inside of his house, Mia should have refused to go up the stairs to use the bathroom; she should have held off and had him to stop her by a local McDonald's or another public place. The closer she got to his bedroom, the less likely she was to leave that house a chaste woman.

4. She shouldn't have gone into his bedroom. She should have headed down the stairs and insisted that he bring the album with him, after all, it wasn't bolted down in his bedroom.

5. Mia should not have sat on the bed. Sitting on a man's bed is pretty much, in his mind, your way of agreeing to have sex with him. Any "no" you speak at this point is interpreted by him as you playing hard to get.

6. When James kissed Mia, she should have stopped him and immediately left the bedroom.

7. Mia should not have had sex with James, and get this, at any point during the encounter, she could have and should have stopped him. She didn't because she wanted to have sex with him as well.

James was an outright fornicator; Mia was a celibate fornicator. The difference is James hadn't proclaimed to be abstinent. He was just a guy who went to church. Mia, on the other hand, had taken a personal mission—she'd planned to remain abstinent until she was married. And while her position was admirable, it wasn't secure. Let me explain.

I coined the term "celibate fornicator" back in 2014 when I recorded a now popular video called "The Reason for the Wait." I'd been stirred or provoked to create this video after one woman who had been trying to take a leadership role in the single women's movement had posted up a status, laughing at how some new guy in her life had picked her up. This hadn't been the first time I'd seen her post about men touching her. It would seem that every few months, there was a new guy in her life, and she'd often post up, joke about and brag about the men being somewhat handsy with her. Of course, she was a Christian and she was not a pastor (thank God). She was just a woman trying to become popular and take a leadership role with today's single women. I didn't know her personally, but somehow, we'd gotten connected on social media. I found myself getting more and more annoyed with her posts because all she talked about was men. It was very clear that she idolized men and marriage, and while this was her issue, what bothered me was that she was encouraging other young women to be as desperate and reckless as she was. Yeah, looking back, I probably should have deleted her, but I didn't, for whatever reason. I didn't read her page, but her posts always came up in my news feed because we had a lot of similar interests and friends. But the day she talked about a guy who hadn't been in her life a full week lifting her body above his head was the day that I grabbed my digital voice recorder and recorded, "The Reason for the Wait." I was frustrated because I knew that she was about to lead a lot of women into sexual immorality, and for what? Just so that she could create a platform for herself? I was disgusted, but I decided to not go against her in my message, but to instead, empower the single women of God, warning them to abstain from fornication and to be careful who they followed. To date, that video has nearly three hundred thousand views. But in the video, I used the term "celibate fornicator," and to be honest, it was not an expression I'd ever used before. I'd never even thought of that phrase. It was just a God-moment for me—a time when Heaven's language interrupted my own.

So, what is a "celibate fornicator"? In short, it is a man or a woman who has taken, either silently or publicly, a vow of abstinence, without understanding God's heart as it relates to purity. What this means is the person is not agreeing to be abstinent because he or she loves the Lord; people who are "abstinent fornicators" or "celibate fornicators" agree to be abstinent for four reasons:

1. They know that sex outside of marriage is a sin.
2. They are being transactional with God, meaning, they are convinced that if they obey God's commands as it relates to sexual purity, that He'll reward them with a

spouse.
3. They are surrounded by others who've taken a vow of purity.
4. They're trying something new.

This means that they have not yet matured; they have not yet fully embraced their God-given identities and they lack knowledge in regards to the purpose of marriage. The space between a question and an answer is called a process. During the process, we are always tempted to fill in the blank or, better yet, answer the question for ourselves. So, when we say, for example, "Lord, send me the man of God that you have for me," this sounds like a statement or, at least it is in the western world. But in truth, this isn't a statement, it's more of a question. The question is, "Lord, why am I still single?" The question is posed, and a process begins. During the process, we are still commanded to follow God's instructions; during the process, we are more tempted to sin against God than any other time. This is because unanswered questions are a burden within themselves. And the trick of the enemy is to keep mounting on more questions until we reason within ourselves that God is simply ignoring us. We start questioning how long it will be before God rewards us for our obedience, why some of our Christian friends have sinned and gotten blessed in the process, and we question if God is mad at us about something. As the questions continue to mount, we slowly, passively, progressively and indiscreetly begin to loosen the screws our boundaries. Before long, the celibate fornicator's chastity belt is just one conversation away from falling. In layman's terms, a celibate fornicator is a fornicator masquerading as an abstinent man or woman of God. This doesn't' mean that they are bad, hell-bound people who are intentionally trying to trick God's people. No. Many of them are just as deceived as the people they deceive, after all, deceived people deceive people. They are immature believers who are mimicking what they think abstinence is, and they are often able to pull off the feat of abstaining for several years. But a pervert will always expose them because people who have no boundaries are masters at finding people whose boundaries are nothing but mirages or people with fluid boundaries. Slaves know how to identify other folks who are in bondage! This makes me think about something a man said to me back in 2009. He said, "I see it in your eyes." I was a married woman living in Germany, but I was designing graphics and websites for ministries at that time. This guy referred to himself as a "sex minister" and he'd hired me to design some graphics for him, but in speaking with him, I could tell that lust had a strong hold on his mind because he'd kept making "careful" advances toward me. He'd said, "I want to get to know you better," in the most lustful tone imaginable. When I'd questioned him, he kept saying, "I see it in your eyes." I didn't know what "it" was, but I was sure that he was speaking of lust. And he was right. I was a faithful woman to the man I'd married, but that didn't mean I was free. I'd just placed some boundaries around myself that would disable me from sinning against the man whose surname I shared, but the woman behind those boundaries needed knowledge, understanding and deliverance. I kept questioning him, trying to get him to outright say what he meant because I could clearly see that he was making advances, but he was playing it safe with the way he did it. After I got him to be more blatant, I rebuked him and ended our working relationship. But get this, Satan was simply pointing out something that belonged to him—something that he saw lodged up in the depths of my soul. I was a lust-filled woman, even though I was Christian. As a matter of fact, I'd sinned to get the man I was married to. Was I a true Christian? Yes! I loved the Lord and I wanted to please Him, but I was also an immature Christian. This was made clear through the fact that I'd attempted to hijack the will of God and climb my way into marriage illegally. I wasn't willing to wait on God because I was immature and I knew what I wanted. I wanted a husband, children and a secure future with my newfound family. This was my ultimate destination at that time; this was my god. But YAHWEH wasn't having it! There was no way that He was going to stand by idly and watch me make a mockery of Him. There was no way that He was going to let me stand before His people with a hijacked marriage.

God has given us the responsibility of guarding our hearts, presenting our bodies as a living sacrifice (holy and acceptable to Him) and loving our neighbors as we love ourselves. All of these responsibilities are burdens, and they force us to create boundaries and to enforce them. Creating boundaries is one challenge, but enforcing those boundaries is where the real test begins. Think of it this way. You reason within yourself that you're going to sell your car for $11,000 and you're not going to allow someone to talk you down on your price. The car is worth $13,000, so asking for $11,000 is more than fair. You place the car up for sale on Craigslist, and you get a few low-ball offers. Nevertheless, you're determined to stand your ground, so you refuse them and keep posting up new ads about your car. Three months later, your car still hasn't sold, and you desperately want to sell it so that you can buy a new car. You finally come across the car that you want, and the seller is asking $16,500 for it. You have $8,000 in your account, and you'd plan to spend no more than $17,000 on your new vehicle. If you sell your old car for $11,000, you'd only have to take $5,500 out of your account, leaving yourself $2,500 to get your tags and insurance. Nevertheless, no one seems to be interested in your ads but scammers.

One day, a man calls you about the car. "I'll give you $9,000 for it. That's all I have. Take it or leave it." He gives you no room for negotiation. Desperate, you try to stand by your price, but he manages to wear you down. A few days later, he hands you an envelope full of cash. You count it, and it's $9,000 like he said. You then sign over the car's title to him and hand him the keys. You'd set a price, but you hadn't enforced it because you allowed yourself to be tempted by another offer. Two weeks later, you see the same car that you just paid $17,000 for on sale for $12,000, and get this, the ad was posted by the guy who talked you down on your price! This is exactly what happens when we fail to enforce our boundaries. We end up feeling robbed of God's promises for us or, at minimum, severely delayed. This is all because we didn't mind establishing the boundaries, but enforcing them, especially in heated moments of temptation, is a job within itself!

What is the burden of boundaries? It's the responsibility that we all have as both mature or immature believers to uphold the love, integrity and sacredness of the Word of God. It's the responsibility to forsake fitting in for the sake of standing out. It is the role and the keys entrusted to us by God to be living examples that He can place on a pedestal and bless. King David called this pedestal a table in Psalm 23:5; it reads, "Thou preparest a table before me in the presence of mine enemies: thou anointest my head with oil; my cup runneth over." What I've learned is that this scripture isn't there to reference the table, it's referencing the seat. And the people at the table are important as well. Contrary to popular belief, this scripture has nothing to do with the mocking of one's enemies; it's not God's way of giving you a moment to "shine" in front of dull people. No. When God puts you at a table or, better yet, on a pedestal, He's doing this so that you can become an example to the people whose hearts are turned away from Him. He wants to honor you so that He can save them, not mock them!

In short, God wants to raise up people who are willing to be templates for others to pattern themselves after. If you are

193

willing to take on this responsibility, please understand that the journey looks a lot easier than it really is, but if you surround yourself with the right people, fill yourself with the Word of God and make up your mind that you're willing to give God every ounce of your heart, He will begin to bless and empower you, but not before drawing a whole other set of boundaries around you. The men (or women) who once looked your way will see you as unattainable. The old friends will walk away, making way for new friends. And more importantly, God won't just give you a new burden, He'll give you the wisdom to lift that burden, for example, you'll set some rules and guidelines around yourself, and you'll use these guidelines as tools of discernment. Should someone try to get you to abandon your morals or make you feel guilty about not being like other Christians, you'll be able to readily identify that person as a weapon formed against you, maybe even a narcissist. And while you may not date like other people, hang out like other people or be invited to most of the events that your peers are hosting, you'll also have a different testimony than theirs. You won't always be nursing a broken heart or standing in somebody's clinic, nervously waiting on the doctor to reappear with your test results. Lastly, you won't feel the need to provoke God to wrath whenever your sin doesn't pan out the way you imagined it would. You'll live a life free of guilt and shame; a life free of ungodly soul ties and idolatry. This is the value of boundaries; it's also the burden of boundaries. It's the same burden that Ahab forsook when he put a crown on Jezebel's head (the equivalent of a wedding ring) and the same burden that Solomon took for granted when he married a bunch of pagan women. It's the same boundaries that David crossed to get to Bathsheba—boundaries that caused him to unleash a generational curse in his family that would leave a trail of lust-filled sin leading from one generation to the next.

Remember this:
1. Yeah, everyone's doing it, but that doesn't mean that you can.
2. Sure, everyone's listening to it, but it doesn't mean that you can.
3. Of course, everyone's watched it, but this doesn't mean that you can.
4. Yes, they'll call you religious, but that doesn't mean that you are.

You're burdened and that's not a bad thing. If your burden is to do the will of God, please know that your burden isn't a curse; it's a heavy blessing. It'll keep you from doing like Ahab; that is, bringing a narcissist into something sacred, thinking that a blessing will somehow come from your decision. Just remember this—there are people out there who would fast for 40 days and 40 nights to carry the burden that you take for granted. This is because what you see as a burden, they see as a blessing!

The Psychology and Biology of Boundaries

Our bodies are interesting, but complex worlds that work very much like the world we live in. Covered by an outer layer of skin, our bodies come equipped with their own personal rivers (blood), highways (nerves and veins), ruler (heart), military (white blood cells) and so on, all of which come together to form a system. In this system, there are many sub-systems at work, all of which are synchronized for our benefit. Our bodies are fighting every day to stay alive, but we aren't necessarily partnering up with our bodies to make their jobs easier; we don't always make it easy for our bodies to function. Instead, we often eat foods that our bodies have to fight, some people engage in premarital sex, so their bodies are always battling with disease and infection and some people attack their own bodies with drugs and alcohol. Some people stay in abusive relationships, hoping that their significant or insignificant others will eventually learn to truly love them, while some just love the sin they're in. Romans 6:23 reads, "For the wages of sin is death; but the gift of God is eternal life through Jesus Christ our Lord."

Yes, sin attacks our bodies. The Bible tells us so. It gets into our bloodstream and begins to pervert the system of our bodies. When a system is perverted, it creates what doctors and society refer to as addictions; this is what the church refers to as strongholds. God gave us instructions designed to help us promote the health, longevity and the soundness of our minds and bodies, but many of us are still nibbling on forbidden fruits, hoping to become our own gods (not necessarily by title, but in deed). Sure, we're Christian, but something in us wants what we cannot have; something in us craves the pleasures that sin affords us. Of course, we definitely don't want the consequences of sin, just the perks and the pleasures. So, we're always waging war against the lusts of our flesh, and we don't always use wisdom in our dealings. If and when we don't institute and enforce boundaries in our lives, it is only a matter of time before we end up in a stronghold.

Google's Online Dictionary defines the word "stronghold" as:
1. a place that has been fortified so as to protect it against attack.
2. a place where a particular cause or belief is strongly defended or upheld.

This will all make sense as you venture deeper into this chapter.

In Christian context, strongholds can be either good or bad, but the word in itself is often used to reference a pattern of thoughts and behaviors that produce short term pleasure, followed by long term pain. These thoughts and behaviors are either generationally, culturally, religiously or personally centered. Strongholds have everything to do with the mind; it's (in a sense) a lock placed on the mind that disables it from maturing or thinking outside of a certain realm. The person in question becomes shortsighted, focusing on the stimuli produced when a certain action or conversation is engaged, but ignoring the long-term effects of their decisions or words. And the person does this repeatedly, meaning, it is a system in the person's life. It is a habit. A great way to describe a stronghold in modern-day language is to think of a computer. Computers have operating systems that have to be updated and upgraded. There are several reasons for this, a couple of them being:

1. To enhance the performance of a computer.
2. To protect computers from hackers, viruses and other enemies of the system. Hackers are usually perverted geniuses. Whatever Microsoft or Apple builds, a hacker, if given enough time, will learn to penetrate. So, technology companies like Microsoft, Apple, Google and IBM have to stay ahead of their enemies by constantly updating their systems and learning from every attack that successfully penetrates their systems.
3. To increase the performance of your operating system.

A stronghold is like a virus on a computer, disabling it from receiving updates and upgrades, thus, making it more vulnerable to more attacks and causing the computer to run extra slowly. It pretty much makes a computer more of a burden than it is a blessing. There are strongholds that manifest themselves physically, strongholds that manifest themselves mentally, strongholds that manifest themselves financially, strongholds that manifest themselves socially and strongholds that manifest themselves spiritually. Below, you'll find a few examples:

Physical Manifestation	Obesity, Anorexia, Bulimia
Mental Manifestation	Depression, Suicidal Thoughts, Unforgiveness
Financial Manifestation	Poverty, Overspending, Fear of Spending (Frugality)
Social Manifestation	Isolation, Unhealthy Co-dependencies
Spiritual Manifestation	Demonic Bondage, Witchcraft

All of the aforementioned pointers are ways that strongholds manifest themselves. Nevertheless, make no mistake about it, strongholds have everything to do with the mind. It is the result of a compromised heart (mind). God told us in Proverbs 4:23, to keep or, better yet, guard our hearts, because out of it flows the issues of life. Understand this: we are three-dimensional beings. Each of us are a spirit, we have a soul and we live in a body (Source: Apostle Bryan Meadows). The soul is comprised of our minds, wills and emotions. Our minds (hearts) are broken up into three parts: conscious, subconscious and unconscious.

1. **Conscious Mind:** This is the first dimension or entry

way into your heart! This is what you're aware of at any given moment; it's what's currently engaging your mind. This could be someone looking at you from across the room, someone talking to you through your phone or a social media post that you're reading. Of course, you're reading this book, so right now, your conscious mind is being engaged. Your imaginations also engage your conscious mind. Again, this as the waiting room of the heart.

2. **Subconscious Mind:** This is the second dimension of the heart! This is our response center. The subconscious mind is where we store and retrieve data that we can readily access. This is the part of your mind that you control; this is the epicenter of our decisions.

3. **Unconscious Mind:** This is the third dimension of the heart! The unconscious mind is our memory banks; it's where we store memories and traumas. The minute you believe something, it makes its way to your unconscious mind and begins to integrate itself into your system. The unconscious mind operates without your permission, for example, your breathing is controlled by your unconscious mind.

So, how does a stronghold affect the heart? Let's first get a biblical understanding of what a stronghold looks like. In the biblical era (mostly Old Testament), kings would often attack territories in an attempt to take their cities; they'd either bring the citizens under submission to their kingdoms or they'd kill off all the citizens (sometimes, just the men) and just take over the territory. But to do this, they had to engage in warfare. Warfare is not the act of war; it is the tactical planning of war. The highest ranking and most intelligent military officials would often gather together and discuss the circumference of a nation, the strengths of that nation and the weaknesses of that nation. They would also discuss what they believed their nation would stand to gain by attacking the other nation. If they decided that attacking the nation would be of major benefit to them, and if they believed that they could overcome that nation, they'd begin planning their attacks, oftentimes without their opponents' knowledge. One of the most effective strategies was to place a stronghold around that city. Now, there are two types of strongholds that you need to be aware of as it relates to the makeup of war. Cities would often build their own strongholds; these were the walls surrounding a city, designed to protect them from being easily attacked. This process or stronghold was called fortification. There were men who would stand on and around the walls so that they could see their enemies approaching from a distance; this was called a garrison. This is an example of a beneficial or a good stronghold; it was designed by the king's officials to protect that particular nation. Next, there is the not-so-good stronghold. This is when a nation would surround a city in an attempt to stop it from trading with other nations and to prevent the citizens from venturing outside of the walls of that city. This type of stronghold was called a siege. Of course, this method of attack was only effective if the nation under siege depended largely on trading with other nations or if there were some resources that the people needed that were outside of the cities' walls. This type of warfare required planning and patience because it could (and did) often backfire. It was designed to cause the city to go into famine and, in some instances, drought. The military and the people would begin to weaken, and after so many months, or in some cases, years, the opposing military would be able to take the city. Again, this did occasionally backfire whenever the city under attack had everything they needed within their walls and did not rely on other nations. The opposing military would begin to starve and weaken, or in some cases, a nation defending the nation under attack would surround the soldiers that were surrounding the city, thus, creating a stronghold around them. Nevertheless, this was a very effective war tactic.

Now, let's look at the psychology of a stronghold and how it affects the heart. God told us to guard our hearts; in other words, to fortify our minds. How do we do this?

1. **By surrounding ourselves with Godly people.** (1 Corinthians 15:33: Be not deceived: evil communications corrupt good manners.)
2. **By obeying the Word of God at all costs.** (James 4:7: Submit yourselves therefore to God. Resist the devil, and he will flee from you.)
3. **By placing God on the front lines of our minds.** (Matthew 6:33: But seek ye first the kingdom of God, and his righteousness; and all these things shall be added unto you.)

4. **By examining our fruits.** (Galatians 5:19-24: Now the works of the flesh are manifest, which are these; adultery, fornication, uncleanness, lasciviousness, Idolatry, witchcraft, hatred, variance, emulations, wrath, strife, seditions, heresies, envyings, murders, drunkenness, revellings, and such like: of the which I tell you before, as I have also told you in time past, that they which do such things shall not inherit the kingdom of God. But the fruit of the Spirit is love, joy, peace, longsuffering, gentleness, goodness, faith, Meekness, temperance: against such there is no law. And they that are Christ's have crucified the flesh with the affections and lusts.)

5. **Through prayer and fasting.** (Matthew 17:21: Howbeit this kind goeth not out but by prayer and fasting.)

6. **By wearing the whole armor of God.** (Ephesians 6:11-17: Put on the whole armour of God, that ye may be able to stand against the wiles of the devil. For we wrestle not against flesh and blood, but against principalities, against powers, against the rulers of the darkness of this world, against spiritual wickedness in high *places*. Wherefore take unto you the whole armour of God, that ye may be able to withstand in the evil day, and having done all, to stand. Stand therefore, having your loins girt about with truth, and having on the breastplate of righteousness; And your feet shod with the preparation of the gospel of peace; Above all, taking the shield of faith, wherewith ye shall

be able to quench all the fiery darts of the wicked. And take the helmet of salvation, and the sword of the Spirit, which is the word of God.

7. **By watching and praying.** (Ephesians 6:18: Praying always with all prayer and supplication in the Spirit, and watching thereunto with all perseverance and supplication for all saints.)

8. **Through unity.** (Ecclesiastes 4:12: And if one prevail against him, two shall withstand him; and a threefold cord is not quickly broken.)

9. **Through community.** (Ephesians 26:8: And five of you shall chase an hundred, and an hundred of you shall put ten thousand to flight: and your enemies shall fall before you by the sword.)

10. **Through praise and worship.** (2 Chronicles 20:22: And when they began to sing and to praise, the LORD set ambushments against the children of Ammon, Moab, and mount Seir, which were come against Judah; and they were smitten.)

11. **Through giving.** (Malachi 3:10: Bring ye all the tithes into the storehouse, that there may be meat in mine house, and prove me now herewith, saith the LORD of hosts, if I will not open you the windows of heaven, and pour you out a blessing, that there shall not be room enough to receive it.)

12. **By casting down strongholds or vain imaginations.** (2 Chronicles 10:3-6: For though we walk in the flesh, we do not war according to the flesh. For the weapons of our warfare are not carnal but

mighty in God for pulling down strongholds, casting down arguments and every high thing that exalts itself against the knowledge of God, bringing every thought into captivity to the obedience of Christ, and being ready to punish all disobedience when your obedience is fulfilled.)

13. **By repenting.** (2 Chronicles 7:14: If my people, which are called by my name, shall humble themselves, and pray, and seek my face, and turn from their wicked ways; then will I hear from heaven, and will forgive their sin, and will heal their land.)

We guard ourselves against strongholds by being watchful, prayerful and obedient to God's Word. We also do this by surrounding ourselves with Godly people (this is our garrison) and by being mindful of what we allow into our ear-gates and eye-gates.

Satan likes to place a siege around the mind of a person, whereas, that person can't seem to venture (in thought) outside of a certain realm. The individual is surrounded on every side by ignorant people. (This isn't an offensive statement; it simply means that (some) information is present, but the people are too blind or disinterested to partake of it, therefore, they ignore it. It means to be naive by choice. And get this, you will never crave anything you've never partook of. Sure, you can try new things, but the majority of people who've been oppressed don't venture outside of the walls of oppression. They build communities, start families and settle down in their oppression. All the same, Satan keeps information out of certain regions and out of certain communities to ensure that they remain impoverished, unlearned and impotent. For example, slave-owners forbade the slaves under their care from learning how to read. They intentionally kept their slaves away from information. "My people are destroyed for lack of knowledge" (Hosea 4:6). All the same, I grew up in Mississippi, a state that has a long history of racial segregation, oppression and hatred. The high school that I attended as a young woman ended up filing a lawsuit against the district (I believe) because the student population of my school was primarily African Americans. There were three schools in our district that were under our superintendent. One of those schools under his care was comprised primarily of Caucasian American students. It had been discovered that all of the textbooks at my school were old and outdated, whereas, the schools that had primarily Caucasian students had new textbooks. I think this may have come to light when one of the other schools petitioned for newer textbooks, so they decided to give our school their old textbooks. I'm not sure of the outcome of that lawsuit, but it is a prime example of a demonic stronghold. This is a stronghold called oppression. This is when information is withheld with the intent of keeping a community, family, or nation from empowering themselves. This allows the offenders to feed the people whatever information they want to feed them and keep the oppressed away from anything or anyone who could educate them.

Demonic oppression is still very much a much-used warfare tactic to date. A few of the ways that Satan keeps people ignorant is through:

1. **Offense.** Proverbs 18:19 states, "A brother offended is harder to be won than a strong city: and their contentions are like the bars of a castle." Trying to get the truth to an offended person is nearly impossible because he or she questions your motives, your integrity and your intentions. And they are not always offended with you! Meaning, you will come across people who are offended with other folks, but just because you look like the people they don't like, they'll look for fault in you.

2. **Social retardation.** This simply means that a person is only used to a certain mindset, so for this reason, the person doesn't know how to be culturally diverse. As a result, the person in question creates a stronghold of his or her own, surrounding himself or herself with people who the individual can relate to. This means that no new information gets into that person or group's heart, therefore, they settle into friendships that are the equivalent of strongholds.

3. **Isolation.** Satan knows the power of two. Or three. Or twelve. Or three hundred. And for this reason, he has driven many people into isolation by causing them (during their eras of immaturity) to open up their lives to what psychologists refer to as the narcissistic personality. After many years and a few encounters with the Jezebel spirit (the spiritual term for a

narcissist), a lot of people isolate themselves and begin to fear having relationships with other people.

4. **Marginalization.** Merriam Webster defines marginalization as: "to relegate to an unimportant or powerless position within a society or group." This is exactly what I described having happened with the school I'd attended. Here's a snippet from an article I read. "Imagine if you were ten years old and already knew your educational choices were limited and your future job prospects dim. This is the situation for children in Germany from Turkish, Kurdish, or Arab backgrounds. Their routine placement in the lowest level schools at a young age determines, for many, the course of their lives. The German school system has traditionally been highly stratified, with students attending Gymnasium (the highest-level school preparing students for university studies), Realschule (the intermediate level), or Hauptschule (the lowest level, which prepares children for work or vocational training). These days, a Hauptschule education most often leads to unemployment or, at best, a low-income job with little hope of career advancement. Evidence demonstrates that children of Turkish, Kurdish or Arabic backgrounds—known as 'migrant' children in Germany even if they are the second or even third generation of immigrants—wind up in disproportionate numbers in the lowest level Hauptschule, condemning them to a cycle of marginalization." As you can see, marginalization is more often than not linked with

racism, and whether we care to admit it or not, racism is still a very large part of American culture.

5. **Division.** There's power in unity, which could only mean that division or disunity is draining. Satan is always dividing families, communities, churches and nations. For example, my family was largely divided before I was born, and they had been divided by religious beliefs and blatant sin. On one side of the spectrum, there were the family members who loved their sin and wanted nothing to do with God, even though they would embrace the concept that He existed and acknowledge Him as God whenever hardships came their way. On the other side of the spectrum were extremely legalistic family members who were provoked by everything, from nail polish to women wearing pants. The religious ones thought they were doing the will of God by separating themselves from the "heathenistic" ones and the sinners just kept on going deeper into the dark trenches of sin. The ones who did embrace God had so much religious residue that they didn't know how to go back and preach the gospel to the rest out of fear of being taken advantage of. Through division, Satan is able to cut off the lines of communication between people, thus disallowing people who are impoverished and uneducated from receiving the truth of God's Word. Think of it this way. Imagine a long line that fell down from Heaven and went through every family and community, allowing the people to hear the truth. Now,

imagine in some places where that line had been cut because of offense and division. This is what division looks like to Heaven.

6. **Desperation.** The hardest man to trust is a hungry one! And I'm not talking about a man who's hungry for revelation or hungry for change, I'm talking about a man who lacks provision! When the demands are not met in a man's life, it produces a level of desperation that causes him to, in a sense, prostitute himself. This is what lack does; this is what poverty does! When a family, for example, has been generationally constricted by poverty, you will begin to see criminals emerging from that family. It's hard to reason with a desperate man, and if he does listen to you, it's because he feels that you can supply him with his basic needs. If you do not and cannot, you lose his ears and he'll turn his attention to someone else. And get this, desperation doesn't always reference the behaviors provoked by an immediate need; desperation is often provoked by a repeated need. A single mother knows that her children will have to eat again, even if they are seated at this moment in front of a buffet. For this reason, she's desperate, even when her children are full. And her desperation doesn't always manifest itself as begging or stealing; for some women, this desperation manifests itself in their willingness to have sex outside of marriage, even to men they are not physically, mentally or spiritually attracted to.

7. **Fornication.** Fornication is a system that moves counterclockwise to marriage. Remember, what happened in the Old Testament era when a man illegally laid down with a woman and was caught. The couple was forced to marry, and because the man pretty much stole his wife from her father, he would automatically pick up a bad name. This was the recipe for poverty, as the Jewish community would no longer trust him or the members of his family to do business. No integral man or woman would allow their daughters or their sons to intermarry into that family, meaning, the sons would have to marry women from other families that had been ostracized and the daughters would have to marry men from questionable families. This was the picture of a generational curse! Get this. Satan still encourages men to steal women to this date, knowing full-well that the large majority of those men will not stick around to raise their offspring. So, the children grow up battling rejection, abandonment and the insecurities that come with the duo. Couples date or court, and temptation enters the picture. But God is our Father. He too wants a bride price, but He wants the potential bride and groom to give him an offering of their hearts and their bodies. Romans 12:1 states, "I beseech you therefore, brethren, by the mercies of God, that ye present your bodies a living sacrifice, holy, acceptable unto God, which is your reasonable service."

8. **Crabs-in-a-bucket mentality.** One of the phrases

that I heard a lot growing up was, "That person thinks they are better than us." I don't remember hearing this from my parents, but I do remember hearing this from just about everyone else around me. They were referring to relatives who'd acquired a certain measure of success and were no longer in touch with the rest of the family. I remember being upset with a few relatives, thinking about how I wouldn't let money change me if I were to get it. Oh, how ignorant I was! Money doesn't change people; people change, and when they do, they begin to attract money. Relatives who hadn't been active in their lives for years suddenly started trying to re-enter their lives the minute the successful relatives' success or pending success had become public knowledge, and when they weren't allowed to, they would typically say that the person in question was high-minded and thought they were better than everyone else. This mentality is promoted, and it causes the children of a family to despise wealth and all of its trappings. For this reason, anytime a person in my family even looked like they were going to be successful, that person would be mocked, bullied and constantly reminded of his or her flaws. At one point, I thought it was just my family who were like that; that is, until I started growing in the Lord and getting delivered from impoverished thinking. I lost more friends in that era than anything! I would someday discover that I'd taken the road less traveled away from poverty, and what I'd endured was a classic "crabs-in-a-bucket" attack. And of course, there are levels to this type of attack, as well.

9. **False religions or leadership.** Leaders of false religions and movements fear that the members of their organizations will get empowered through the reading of the Word of God and through healthy, Godly discipleship. To keep this from happening, they'll oftentimes isolate the people in their organizations or movements, telling them that it was the will of God for them to distance themselves from any and everyone who did not agree with their mission. The people are led to believe that outsiders are enemies and they are fed only the information that's given to them; they are intentionally and strategically kept away from any information that would empower them or cause them to question the leaders' authority. A great example of this type of stronghold is what we see happening with North Korea. Kim Jong-un, the "supreme leader" of North Korea, is a dictator who rules with an iron thumb by fixing elections, limiting (oftentimes prohibiting) access to the Internet and by controlling what the people watch on television. The government controls the media. And as far as religion goes, Wikipedia reports the following, "Officially, North Korea is an atheist state. There are no known official statistics of religions in North Korea. According to Religious Intelligence, 64.3% of the population are irreligious,

16% practice Korean shamanism, 13.5% practice Chondoism, 4.5% are Buddhist, and 1.7% are Christian. Freedom of religion and the right to religious ceremonies are constitutionally guaranteed, but religions are restricted by the government. Amnesty International has expressed concerns about religious persecution in North Korea" (Wikipedia/North Korea/Religion). The population of North Korea is 25 million. If two percent are believers, this means that to date, 24,500,000 souls are not saved! Think about this! The citizens are not allowed to leave the country without permission and public executions are the regime's way of striking fear in the hearts of the people. Of course, we see this behavior, not just in North Korea, but on some religious fronts.

10. **Religiousness.** Religiousness is one of the hardest strongholds to penetrate. Think of it this way. If a man has been told his entire life that every person outside of his denomination is a hell-bound heathen, and the only way they could be saved is by worshiping God the way his church worships God, it is hard to get through to that man. This is because he genuinely believes that in order to have and exercise faith, he has to hold onto the lies that he was taught and that Satanically bound people disguising themselves as Christians would someday approach him and try to lead him astray. So, when someone attempts to save him with the truth, he doesn't consider what's being said; instead, he proclaims a bunch of well-rehearsed

lines in his attempt to prove himself to his pastor and God. Now, religiousness doesn't always mean that people have a leader, it means that somewhere in the ancestral pool, one of the matriarchs or patriarchs of the family submitted themselves to a false religion, false doctrine or an extremely legalistic church. The family continued to believe whatever it was that they were taught, even if their religious organization closed its doors. People who come out of legalistic churches or families often have a very difficult time settling into healthy churches. Instead, they tend to be very judgmental, critical and fearful.

11. **Bad associations/ Gossip.** I want you to imagine this scenario. God empowers a woman named Jane with wisdom that another woman (we'll call her Amy) needs. Jane has survived a lot of hardships and she's grown to become a very integral and relatively wealthy woman. Amy, on the other hand, has been praying for God to deliver her from poverty and help her to provide for her three children. Jane and Amy work for the same company, but they've never said much to one another. This is because one of their co-workers, Hilda, who is a friend of Amy's doesn't like Jane. So, she has badmouthed Jane to Amy, telling her that she doesn't trust Jane because she has "beady eyes," plus, she claims that she's heard that Jane likes to sleep around with married men. This isn't true, but Amy accepts the report and intentionally keeps her distance from Jane. But the problem is,

Jane and Amy have crossed paths for a reason; God set it up that way. Jane isn't working at the company for money, she's simply interning at the company. Amy makes it her personal mission to avoid Jane as much as she can, even taking the stairs to avoid running into Jane on the elevator. One day, Jane finishes her internship and leaves the company. Amy cries out to God again, begging Him for the money to pay her bills. Hilda, on the other hand, tells a few coworkers that Amy is an unfit mother who can barely keep her lights on. Do you see how bad association and gossip stood between Amy and the answer to her prayers? Sometimes, God wraps His "yes" and "amen" up in flesh, and He sends these people into our arenas so that they can deliver His Word to us. Now, the words they share aren't always prophetic; sometimes, God wants them to share their stories with us so that we'll be encouraged and we'll avoid the many snares that they once fell into. Nevertheless, the enemy works tirelessly to keep people apart; he does this through gossip and cliquish behavior. Sadly enough, people have prayed for something or someone to manifest for years, only to have the answers to their prayers standing just a few feet away from them. However, to get to these blessings, they have to humble themselves and close off their ears to negativity.

12. **Demonic interference.** The prophet Daniel fasted for three weeks to receive an answer from God. An angel

came three weeks later and told him that he (the angel) had been sent to deliver the answer to Daniel's prayers, but the Prince of Persia (a principality) withstood him. Let's look at the angel's response. Daniel 10:12-13 reads, "Fear not, Daniel: for from the first day that thou didst set thine heart to understand, and to chasten thyself before thy God, thy words were heard, and I am come for thy words. But the prince of the kingdom of Persia withstood me one and twenty days: but, lo, Michael, one of the chief princes, came to help me; and I remained there with the kings of Persia." This was demonic interference, of course. Just like the enemy will use people to oppress other people, Satan uses demonic angels (demons, principalities, rulers) to keep us from hearing back from God. This is why we have to do like Daniel did; we have to fast and pray.

13. **Familiarity.** Sometimes, the people around us (especially our mentors and leaders) have the information that we need to break free from a siege, but because of familiarity, we have trouble receiving this information from the people in our lives. This is silly; it's asinine even, but I've found that some people will make it a personal mission of theirs to get close to someone in leadership. They'll serve the person, give gifts and sing praises about that person, however, if they are given the access that they want, another chemical reaction takes place in their brains—one that is stronger than the one released during the

phases of admiration. They simply do not understand or respect order, meaning, they don't know how to have relationships with people who outrank them in the natural or the spirit. Now, when I say outrank, I'm not saying that the people are better than them, I am saying that the people know better than them. Once familiarity settles into their hearts, they begin to question just about everything their mentor says and does; once familiarity sets in, they become argumentative, competitive and even more manipulative. God then delivers the mentor from the mentee who's trying to oppress him or her, and the mentee goes roaming about like a roaring lion, looking for someone else to admire. This process repeats itself until the mentee becomes bitter and even more convinced that he or she is called to leadership and needs to expose the workers of God. Another name for this spirit is the Absalom spirit. The mentor had what the mentee needed to get him or her free, but in the mentee's world, everyone is equal; there is no rank or protocol.

14. **Through fear.** I took my dog outside for his bathroom break one night. It was really late, but I'd just woken up from a nap. When I went outside, I didn't see the huge wolf spider standing on the threshold of my door. It is possible that he crawled up there after I'd gone outside, but either way, when I turned to go back into my home, I saw a huge, black wolf spider standing in the way, and I wasn't about to walk past

him. I called my dog away from the door and tried to figure out how I was going to get past the spider. I had mace in my hand and I was honestly tempted to mace the spider, but I had to consider the fact that the mace may have lingered and affected me and my dog whenever we tried to walk past it. All the same, it is possible that the mace wouldn't have affected the spider in any way. I then remembered that I was outside, so I walked over to a large tree in the center of my yard and started looking for fallen sticks. I found a medium-sized one and I used it to bat the spider away. Now, get this. I wasn't about to walk past that spider, and I wasn't going to let my dog walk past it either. I had to remove it out of my path so that I could get back into my home. Satan pulls a similar stunt. He places people, objects and memories on our paths that are designed to keep us from entering our next levels. This is why, in order to go to the next level, we have to learn to march past fear or, at least, chase away what's been chasing us.

15. **Through the deployment of comfort zones.**
Comfort zones are often nothing but beautifully decorated prisons that we've invested in for a long period of time. Humans are creatures of habit, and as such, we do not like to go outside of what we know. So, we surround ourselves with people who think like us, look like us and behave like us. We'd rather have relationships where we can talk nonstop, rather than being mentored by someone and having to listen for a

change. We don't mind being bound as long as we're comfortable and we're able to get our needs met, even if we're stretching every dollar, nickel, quarter, dime and penny to pay our bills.

16. **No deliverance ministries in sight.** Growing up, I'd never heard of a deliverance ministry. I'm pretty sure that someone somewhere in my city was performing deliverance, but I'd never heard of them. We didn't have computers back then, so we simply learned to deal with whatever the devil threw at us. To date, there are some regions where the enemy has placed strongholds on the people and kept them far away from anyone who would dare to even mention deliverance to them. There are no deliverance ministries in these regions, only a bunch of religious institutions disguising themselves as churches.

These are just a few of the ways that Satan oppresses God's people or, better yet, builds a siege around them. Just like we have to create boundaries around ourselves, the enemy likes to surround us with lines, borders, boundaries and limitations that he intends to keep us from venturing past. And these restrictions are often very effective, otherwise, he wouldn't use them.

So, how does a stronghold affect our hearts; that is, our conscious, subconscious and unconscious minds? It's simple. By keeping out information that would grow and mature us into the people God designed us to be. When information is kept out of an individual, family, community or region, the people are physically limited to certain neighborhoods, income brackets and jobs. Next, he filters into that individual, family, community or region the information he wants them to have. This is why there are many crime-ridden areas in America. The people are marginalized and a lot of the music and media that was filtered into them promote violence, the objectification of women, promiscuity and pride. This happened until the sounds no longer came from without, they started coming from within!

How does the mind engage in warfare?
1. By refusing to believe something that doesn't sound reasonable.
2. By keeping conversations, suggestions and doctrines in our conscious mind (the waiting room of our souls) as long as possible so that we can consider, test and prove (or disprove) the information.
3. Through imaginations. Some imaginations are good; others are bad. But when we dream of Godly lifestyles outside of the limitations that we are currently living in, we strive to learn more and do better.
4. By not creating soul ties with any and everyone who attempts to make themselves a fixture in our lives. Have you ever had an uneasy feeling about someone? Of course, you have! And that feeling likely saved you a lot of money, a lot of heartache, and in some cases, it probably even saved your life! Every

encounter you've had with people has been beneficial to where you are right now. Yes, even the bad encounters. Especially the bad encounters! This is why we often say things like, "I have a bad feeling about ...." or "Something's not right." What's happening here is your unconscious mind is trying to communicate with your conscious mind to get you to run for your life or, at minimum, for your sanity!

Now, that we understand the psychology of boundaries, let's look at the biology of boundaries. The science behind the mind (psychology) and the science behind the body (physiology) are both interesting because they help us to understand how God works. What takes place in the natural is a reflection of how the spirit realm works. For example, there are levels of intimacy. This is why some people have associates, friends, close friends, and then, best friends. The most intimate of this group (best friend) is typically the friend who knows the most about the person in question. Just as there are levels of intimacy to friendships, there are levels of intimacy regarding romantic relationships. This is why one person is normally referred to as "the love of our lives." This is also why, if you were to watch a paternity show like Paternity Court, you'll see women entering the courtroom with their grown children in tow. The children look angry, rejected and confused (in some cases). The potential father looks confident that the child in question is not his child, but the mother is confident that her son or daughter was fathered by the defendant. The court proceedings begin and both parties (the defendant and the plaintiff) tell two very different versions of the same story. The mother is angry but poised as she details what she thought was a thriving relationship. The potential father stands just a few feet away with a smirk on his face. In that moment, he looks like an arrogant, immature deadbeat father who's gone out of his way to avoid paying child support. "Tell the defendant how hard it was for you to raise this child on your own," Judge Lauren Lake says to the mother who, by now, has gotten even more emotional. A few minutes later, the son or daughter begins to speak. (For example's sake, let's say it was a son.) He rubs his mother's back as a show of support before speaking. He's angry but hardened. Every mother in the audience wants to run out of her seat and hug him before taking a detour in the defendant's direction and beating him within an inch of his life. But if you were to listen carefully to the testimonies, you'd hear the real story by taking snippets of what the mother said and snippets of what the potential father said, and here's what you'll come to realize. The mother was in love with the guy, so much so that she'd never gotten over him. He wasn't the per-se "love of her life," but he was the most handsome and most evasive man she's ever had an encounter with. He wasn't willing to commit to her, but she was committed to nabbing him. Nevertheless, the month she'd met him, she was already involved in a sexual relationship with another man. She'd promptly ended that relationship, in some cases, to pursue the "eye candy" that she was now standing next to in the courtroom. She'd told everyone who'd listened that the man was, without a shadow of doubt, the father of her son. She'd done this to impress them. She wanted everyone to know that the good-looking guy with the head full of hair had been in a relationship with her, a relationship she claims was brief but passionate —one he claims was nothing more than a sexual relationship. "Your Honor, I've never even took this woman on a date!" the potential father shouts out in his attempt to make it very clear to the judge and everyone watching that he had not had a "boyfriend/girlfriend" type relationship with the plaintiff. Moments later, the results are read. "When it comes to 26-year-old, _____, Mr. Doe, you are NOT the father!" The mother's facial expression suddenly changes. Shame and guilt suddenly replace anger. "That's not possible!" she shouts over the roars of the crowd. The mother, accuser and plaintiff had not been honest with her child, but the question that remains is why? Because she'd held the man, the potential father, the defendant at such high regard. Love doesn't have to be present for intimacy to take place. Whenever a human gives another human a highly regarded, sacred place in their hearts, they have just brought that person into an intimate place which means that, to the person in question, the couple are involved in an intimate relationship. To the other person involved in the relationship, it may be nothing more than a casual secret—a means to an end. The man wanted sex. That's it and that's all.

There are levels of intimacy; we've already established this as it relates to our hearts, but the same is true for our bodies and our spirit. One man can casually greet a woman from a distance. One man can hug her in public as a show of brotherhood. One man can call her. But the only man who should be sleeping with her is her husband. These are levels of intimacy, but amazingly enough, each man has the ability to affect her physical health if he has physical access to her. The man who greets her from a distance, because he has little to no physical access to her, cannot affect her life unless they touch the same thing or are connected through people. For example, if he lives with the man who hugs the woman, he can transfer a cold to that man. That man can transfer the cold to the woman. Additionally, the man who hugged her can share his scent with her, whether it's pleasant or unpleasant. He has more intimate access to her than the man who waves from a distance. Now, her husband has another level of intimate access, one that is sacred and should be off limits to everyone else. He gets the most intimate level of access because he's the one who has sex with her. He can give her anything from a child to a sexually transmitted disease to a mild cold. The point is, with every level of intimacy that we share with another human being, we give them more of an ability to impact in our lives, and as such, their choices not only affect our minds, but they can possibly affect our physical health as well. Thankfully, our bodies have a system that is designed to offer us some measure of protection against viruses and bacteria.

Our bodies are always taking us through some form of deliverance. This is our bodies' own version of biological warfare. When something lodges itself in our throats, whether it is food or a pathogen, our throats respond by coughing and pushing the foreign obstacle out of our airways and out through our mouths. When a microorganism tries to enter our eyes, our eyes respond by tearing up. When a foreign particle or pathogen enters our noses, our bodies respond to the perceived attack by causing us to sneeze. This is why it's not always a good idea for us to try and stop a sneeze from taking place. We have to work with our bodies' systems, rather than working against them. But to do this, we have to understand the complex world that is our bodies. For example, we all have white blood cells. Our white blood cells protect us by attacking any pathogen that enters our bodies. Pathogens are disease-causing bacteria, viruses and other microorganisms. Anything that illegally enters our bodies is confronted and attacked by our white blood cells. But our white blood cells aren't our first lines of defense. Our skin is. The skin is the largest organ of our bodies, and it covers and protects every organ. Our mucous membranes also protect us from infection; they are the pink lining in our mouths, noses, throats, eyelids and so on. If a pathogen gets past the skin (through a cut or a membrane) and is able to enter our bloodstream, our white blood cells wage war against that pathogen. Platelets rush to the wounded area to begin the clotting process; this way, we don't bleed to death. This process is called homeostasis. The wound then starts to repair itself and we all aid in the healing process by keeping that area clean and bandaged. Nevertheless, we've all been sick at some point; we all know what it feels like to have a cold, and most of us have experienced the flu. This means that sometimes, our white blood cells are unable to fight off the viruses, bacteria and germs that enter our bodies. This is especially true when our white blood cell count is low. Nevertheless, when we do get sick, our bodies don't just submit to an attack, our white blood cells continue to battle against every foreign agent that attempts to invade it.

As we can all see, our bodies have boundaries, just as God has instructed us to place boundaries around our hearts. John 10:1 is a very interesting verse of scripture. It reads, "Verily, verily, I say unto you, He that entereth not by the door into the sheepfold, but climbeth up some other way, the same is a thief and a robber." This scripture deals with order or, better yet, protocol. People ask all the time, "How do I guard myself against the wrong guy or the wrong friends? 1 John 4:1 answers this question. It states, "Beloved, believe not every spirit, but try the spirits whether they are of God: because many false prophets are gone out into the world." But of course, this only brings about another question. How does one test a spirit? Simply put, pay attention to the door that the person is trying to enter! Let me explain.

I design seals and logos for ministries. I also publish and edit books. And finally, I often teach classes where I'm helping people to overcome some stronghold in their lives. Needless to say, I've worked with thousands of people and I've heard and seen just about everything under the sun. It took me years of frustration, years of being tempted to quit and years of developing and expiring systems before I would learn to master the world of business. At one point, I spent a lot of time complaining about the conditions of people's hearts. I found it difficult to accept that many of my fellow brothers and sisters in Christ were as manipulative as they were. Bitterness started setting in, but I had enough sense to know not to stay there. I kept praying, refused to quit and kept updating my systems. God would give me what I revered as hard instructions—instructions that I feared would close my business. For a season, I was struggling to get orders, and many of the ones I did get came from people who wanted to pay the least but get the most in return. They were unreasonable and unrealistic, to say the least. I remember designing logos for $35 and having clients who would want me to keep revising the logos for weeks and months on end. Of course, I soon realized they didn't know what they wanted, and many of them became addicted to delegation or, at least, that was my take on it. They loved having power over another human being; they loved walking through busy places and calling me in an attempt to make themselves look important. Again, this was, at minimum, what I gathered from many of them, especially the ones who kept asking for silly revisions and only calling me when they were in public arenas. But I could hear God saying for me to take my prices up substantially and to place rules around my business. He was telling me to draw a line in the sand, to add structure to my business and to only allow customers to receive a select amount of revisions for whatever package they chose. At first, I resisted Him because business was already slow. I reasoned within my heart that if I did what the Lord was impressing upon me to do, I would lose the customers I had. I was right. But this wasn't a bad thing. I eventually followed God instructions after a very frustrating event with a customer, and for a season or a few months, business got even slower. At this point, I didn't care anymore because I was tired of working for two and three weeks trying to perfect an already perfect logo for a measly $35 or a seal for a mere $75. I took my prices up initially to $149 and only offered one revision with the $149 package. I listed the new rules on the website, and the order form now required customers to acknowledge that they understood and agreed with the new rules. I got quite a few phone calls from customers who were growing used to taking advantage of me. They wanted to tell me what they wanted over the phone, but I stopped them before they could put a period behind their sentences. I let them know that all of my business was done via the order form; they would have to sign it, pay the required deposit and follow the instructions. Just about every customer I had during that era fled. They loved low prices and no protocol. But during the season of drought, God taught me a lot about business and a lot about myself. I didn't spend that season sulking. Instead, I started designing seals and logos that I would place up on my site for sale. Before long, I started getting orders again, but what stood out to me the most was the fact that the people who were placing orders with me even had a different accent than my former customers. They just sounded wealthy! They weren't slowly navigating through a conversation, trying to talk over me or pretend as if they hadn't heard what I'd said. Instead, they were articulate people who didn't cringe at the $149 price tag. What's crazy is the people I once worked for used to complain about paying $35-$75, asking me if I had anything cheaper. Now, here's a few lessons I've learned over the years. It was in that season that I realized the power of patience, coupled with obedience and diligence.

Your mind has a system. Your body has a system. But do you have a system set up that you utilize every time someone tries to enter your life or move closer to your heart? If you don't, I can almost guarantee you that you've spent a lifetime being emotionally wounded by narcissists. These people are the bacteria and viruses that God is trying to protect us from. And they rarely look or sound troubled; instead, they often disguise themselves as functional and helpful when, in truth, they are toxic. One of the most frequent coaching/counseling sessions I have to perform to this day are with people who either have no boundaries in their lives or people whose boundaries are flexible. And in 99 percent of these cases, the people on the other end of the line are desperately trying to figure out how to protect themselves from being hurt again. Still bleeding from the last emotional heart attack, they've come to realize that they are magnets for narcissists. Everywhere they go, they attract Jezebelic, narcissistic people who come into their lives and wreak havoc. I'll tell you what I often tell them. The narcissist is not at fault for wrecking your life. You see, 1 Peter 5:8

warns us, "Be sober, be vigilant; because your adversary the devil, as a roaring lion, walketh about, seeking whom he may devour." What does this scripture tell us?

1. **It tells us to be sober.** I know that we affiliate this word with intoxication, but in truth, the effects that alcohol and drugs have on the human mind are reminiscent of the effects that lies have on the human mind as well. This is why Apostle Paul asked the Church of Galatia, "O foolish Galatians, who hath bewitched you, that ye should not obey the truth, before whose eyes Jesus Christ hath been evidently set forth, crucified among you?" That term "bewitched" simply means to fascinate, astonish, overwhelm with wonder or to not think soberly. The way Satan intoxicates believers is by doing the very same thing he'd done to Eve in the Garden of Eden. He lies. So, when someone starts filling your heard with sweet nothings, planning a future with you and telling you how important you are to them, your assignment, according to Proverbs 4:23, is to guard your heart, test the spirit (see 1 John 4:1), watch and pray (see Matthew 26:41), submit their words to your multitude of counselors (see Proverbs 11:14), refuse to submit your body in sin (see Romans 12:1) and resist the temptation of the enemy (James 4:7). You're also to allow that person to excuse himself or herself from your life should he or she choose to. You see, Satan needs a sin offering to proceed past your boundaries, and every time you sin, he's able to inch closer and

closer to every level of your heart (conscious, subconscious, unconscious). He wants to build a siege around your heart, one that will make it difficult for you to hear from God; this way, you'll be so desperate for love, desperate to get your needs met and desperate to stay alive that you'll come and submit to his system.

2. **It tells us to be vigilant.** This means to be watchful. Never get so comfortable that you forget that you have an enemy! Satan is both patient and impatient. He wants to take you down as quick as he can, but at the same time, he's a true businessman. Therefore, he's not just focused on you, he thinks in generations. Whatever you don't overcome, your children have to wrestle with. Sadly enough, many children have been overcome by their parents' demons. Pay attention your conversations, your associations and the health of your heart at all times. In short, always be willing to conduct self-inventory. I'm not telling you to be paranoid; I'm simply telling you to monitor your thoughts and your words. For example, I can always tell when it's time for me to go through another round of deliverance because I'll normally start feeling overwhelmed, griping all the time and feeling like I want to change my number and leave the country. When this happens, at first, I'll normally focus on the event that caused me to feel that way, but after a day or two, I'll start paying more attention to myself. I'll pray and wait. It doesn't take me long to decide that I

need deliverance and so, I make it a point to get it.

3. **It tells us that Satan goes about seeking whom he may devour.** This tells me that he cannot touch everyone. He sees boundaries; he knows his limitations! Nevertheless, the saints who love their sin almost always find themselves in the devil's mouth praying for a miracle.

Take a lesson from your heart and your body, and learn to draw boundaries around yourself, and last, but not least, you have to faithfully enforce those boundaries. This is where I messed up in business more than a few times. I wouldn't enforce the boundaries whenever a customer was super nice or making a large purchase. In one hundred percent of the cases where I didn't follow protocol in my business, I ended up having to spend more time and lose more money than normal. And in one hundred percent of the cases where a customer was trying to get around my processes, that customer ended up being problematic. He or she didn't want to go through the door (legal access); instead, the customer opted for the window (illegal access). Nowadays, I enforce the rules in my business and my personal life faithfully. Has this scared away some potential clients? Yes! Has this scared away men who were interested in getting to know me? Absolutely! And get this, I'm glad it did because anytime you enforce a boundary, you are engaging in warfare! And every time a person leaves your life or refuses to get to know you just because that person doesn't like your boundaries, you can rest assured that the individual is a weapon formed against you. All the same, whenever you draw boundaries around yourself and enforce those boundaries, you chase away the devil (see James 4:7).

RESPECTING BOUNDARIES

Zoning. This word has so many meanings and is used in many fields, from retail to real estate. Nevertheless, for the sake of this lesson, we will be looking at zoning as it relates to real estate. The following information was taken from the University of Wisconsin's website:

"Zoning is the way the governments control the physical development of land and the kinds of uses to which each individual property may be put. Zoning laws typically specify the areas in which residential, industrial, recreational or commercial activities may take place" (Source: https://people.uwec.edu/ What is Zoning).

There are different types of zoning in the United States, which include, but are not limited to:

- Residential Zoning
- Commercial Zoning
- Industrial Zoning
- Agricultural Zoning

Each one of these zones is designated space for a specific type of establishment. For example, spaces that are classified as residential are for private residences only. No one can build a business or run a farm in a residential zone unless it is considered a combination zone. Most zones are not combination unless you head towards the outskirts (also known as the country) of a region or, in some cities, the downtown area is often considered a combination zone (it's often a mixture of businesses and homes).

Without zoning laws, a business owner could purchase a building right next to a home that you are buying or have purchased, and that business owner could launch a very loud and seedy club. This would put you and your family in eminent danger, take away your peace and cause the value of your property to drastically decline. So, a house that you paid $500,000 for could suddenly lose its value and be worth a meager $78,000 in a matter of years simply because there were no boundaries, borders or restrictions put in place to protect each system. All the same, a person could build a house next to your business and then start complaining about the loud music and all the traffic, or that person could start harassing the people who patronize your business. Without zoning laws, a false religion could build a church right next door to your home, and you'd find yourself in the middle of a heated religious debate every time you told the members to stop parking in front of your yard. Again, zoning laws, like boundaries, are designed to protect systems. The family structure is a system. Businesses are systems. Religious institutions are systems. The purpose of zoning laws, of course, is to enforce respect for one another. You see, without zoning laws, you could end up purchasing a house, only to find yourself living next to a fish factory. This means that zoning laws have made life so much easier for us. Thankfully, the majority of us have never had to wake up to the smell of raw fish. Now, take this lesson and apply it to the limitations that God has placed on us—limitations that He calls sins. Sure, sin looks and sounds like a loud after-party that none of us wants to miss, but we have to. It is God's will to give us our assignments and our borders, but it is a part of our assignment to respect His will.

Like our municipalities, it is important that we create boundaries around ourselves, our faith, our relationships and our material possessions. What's even more important is that we enforce these boundaries, after all, anyone can create boundaries, but enforcing those boundaries is oftentimes the greatest challenge. When you create boundaries around yourself, you're protecting your sanity, your sanctity, your soberness, your self-esteem and your peace of mind. When you create boundaries around your faith, you are guarding your relationship with God. When you create boundaries around your relationships, you are protecting and preserving your personalized community. When you create boundaries around your material possessions, you are protecting your wealth from the thieves and the cankerworms that would rob you. Every one of these areas is a zone, and you should have rules established around each of these zones. If you don't, you will find yourself having to create them every time one of those areas is visited by a narcissist. Please understand that Satan comes to steal, kill and destroy—but, he doesn't always look, behave or sound like Satan when he comes to do those things. The Bible tells us that he does and will disguise himself as an angel of light (see 2 Corinthians 11:14). You may have found yourself complaining about people not respecting your boundaries, but if you haven't published them, how can they respect what you have not established? Of course, you don't have to create a printout and give it to everyone in your life, but you should at least have boundaries to communicate about. For example, an established boundary of mine is no one can fornicate in my house, including family. As you can imagine, I don't have a lot of traffic at my house because I have rules and because I enforce those rules without fail. I have family members who've verbally communicated with me that they would never want to live with me because of the rules that I have. I have family members who have absolutely nothing to do with me because they cannot and will not associate with anyone who has or enforces rules. This is because some of them have been broken and perverted by the enemy so much that they see anyone who has standards as being high-minded and even controlling. So, whenever I say to a family member who has a boyfriend, "You can come and stay for the weekend, but your boyfriend can't come," this statement sounds offensive to them. I remember some years ago, a relative of mine expressed that she wanted to come to Mississippi (where I was living at the time) and stay with me for about a week just to visit. I agreed. I even offered to purchase her flight for her because she said that she couldn't afford to get one. A few days after we had this discussion, I realized that I needed to have another discussion with her, given the fact that she was always talking to me about some guy that she referred to as her boyfriend. They weren't living together, but I had a feeling that she was planning to bring him with her. So, I called her and let her know that she could not bring the guy with her. She was immediately offended. She told me that they didn't have to sleep in the same bed or the same room, nevertheless, I held my ground. No boyfriends will be snoozing at my house. She then told me that I didn't have to worry about purchasing his flight. She said that she was going to purchase it. Of course, this took me by surprise because she'd told me that she couldn't afford to fly herself out, so I was offering to pay for her, not realizing that she was planning to use her money to fly some strange dude out to my house. Of course, I told her that since she could afford to fly herself out, that she could buy her own ticket. A day or two later, she called me to cancel our plans. I remember her words vividly; she said, "My boyfriend said that we're not going to waste our vacation coming to a place where we can't even sleep together." I agreed with the both of them. "Stay home," I told her and that was that. After that, we haven't had much of a relationship besides an occasional "hey" on social media.

I created boundaries, but the next rule was for me to enforce them. This is why when people book me for coaching and they talk about family members who keep taking advantage of them, my first question is, "What are your boundaries and how are you enforcing them?" Because it's obvious to me that the person has elected to keep family members around at the expense of their boundaries. No way! I would rather keep my boundaries and let people walk out of my life than for me to lift my boundaries and allow the wrong people to stay in my life. Remember, James 4:7 states, "Submit yourselves therefore to God. Resist the devil, and he will flee from you." This means that if I honor God with my life and with my choices, and I resist the enemy's advances, Satan will see me as a threat and run away from me! Yes, even folks who got Satan in them will avoid me!

Create boundaries for others to respect. Please understand that boundaries help you with discernment. You see, only bound people hate boundaries. So, if you communicate a reasonable boundary in your life, and someone tries to go past that boundary, get you to lift that boundary or they leave your life because of that boundary, that person shouldn't be in your life. And of course, don't forget to enforce every boundary that you establish. The right people will respect those boundaries without complaining. As a matter of fact, the right people will also have boundaries drawn around their lives that they'll communicate to you, and because they understand the importance of boundaries, they won't get offended when you talk about your own.

As I mentioned earlier, I recently started watching Judge Judy and it has easily become one of my favorite court shows. If you're not familiar with the show, Judge Judy is a popular court show series, starring Judge Judith Susan Sheindlin. The series displays real cases that are being judged and ruled over by Judge Judy. The reason this show has piqued my interest is because of Judge Judy's no-holds-barred way of getting the information she needs to get to the truth and render a judgment. She has drawn many boundaries in her courtroom, and she enforces them without apology. After being a judge for well over thirty years, she's come to understand human nature, so she uses that knowledge to keep order in her courtroom. In one of her cases, a man went before her to sue his neighbor for a motorcycle that the neighbor had (allegedly) stolen from him. Of course, the neighbor didn't admit to stealing the bike. Instead, he claimed that he'd gotten possession of the bike after purchasing it from a guy he knew. After having been confronted by the cops regarding the motorcycle, the neighbor decided to return the bike to its rightful owner, but the problem is, the motorcycle had been damaged. The case was a clear slam dunk; the man was going to win and the (alleged) thief was going to have to pay up. Judge Judy repeatedly questioned the defendant, not giving him or his girlfriend room to pause between answering her. She knew exactly what it took to expose a liar. But the plaintiff seemed to be on the edge of his seat. He was so determined to tell his story that Judge Judy had to give him one of her infamous "hushes" a few times, and even then, it was clear that he was antsy. He was winning his case without having to say much of anything. Nevertheless, he'd rehearsed the story in his head so much that it was pure torture for him to stand still and remain silent while the judge drilled the defendant. Thankfully for him, the judge ruled in his favor, but I would venture out to say that I think he would have rather told his story at the expense of losing his case, rather than having won and been forced to remain silent. Why is this? Because of unforgiveness. He knew that he'd be coming on national television, and he was overly obsessed with the idea of exposing his thieving neighbor, so-much-so that winning the case was no longer his main objective. It would have been the dessert on his menu, but the main course was humiliating the defendant. This makes me think of how we are with God. Sometimes, God has to "hush" us because we'll talk ourselves right out of a blessing. You see, had Judge Judy allowed the man to have the time he wanted to air out all of his grievances, he would have incriminated himself or said something that would have forced her to render a different judgment, one that was not in his favor. He didn't understand this, so he attempted to slip his story in a few times, only to be silenced by the judge. He was clearly offended, not realizing she was working on his behalf. She placed a boundary in front of the man's lips and would not allow his tongue to cross it. That boundary had purpose backing it. That boundary was clearly there to protect him and help him recover some of the money he'd lost repairing his bike. Again, this is how we are with God. He's given us boundaries, speed limits and restrictions so that He can:

1. Protect us
2. Deliver us
3. Empower us
4. Bless us
5. Equip us

But because we are so focused on what other folks have done to us and taken from us, we become more obsessed with exposing those people than we do with just allowing God to recover all that was stolen from us. I often say this, and while it may be offensive to some, many have used this truth as a gauge to free themselves from unforgiveness. I often say that many women (not all) go after child support, not for the sake of taking care of their children, but they do this to hurt and financially control the man who hurt them. (Remember, hurt people hurt people.) They do this so that he can be reminded of the family he left behind every time he has to pay up. This is why, in some cases, it's not child support; it's nothing short of a medical bill for their broken hearts. In some cases, it's no longer a medical bill for their hearts, it has graduated into the funeral expenses for the dead relationship. Now, **this isn't for every woman who collects child support**, of course. I'm speaking of the select ones who simply cannot have a conversation with their exes without getting upset or bringing up the past. They didn't understand that God had placed a no-touch boundary between the two of them, but they'd both crossed that boundary and given in to the lusts of their flesh. Both parties had an underlying motive. In many cases, the man wanted to engage in a sexual relationship—nothing more. The woman, on the other hand, wanted to get married and start a family—nothing less. Every woman has an invisible price tag hanging on her heart. After listening to her speak or observing her movements, the guy realized that he couldn't afford her, even though she'd discounted herself. In other words, he would have to pay for her love in increments. She wanted to get married and have the family she'd never had growing up. He couldn't afford to give her this because he didn't have enough love, patience, knowledge or maturity to head up a home. Nevertheless, he still wanted to engage in a short-term or long-term sexual relationship with the woman. Not possessing the currency that she desired, he gave her fake currency. He sold her a few dreams, or he led her to believe that their relationship would potentially end in marriage. It hadn't. Instead, it ended three years and two children later. Realizing that she had been robbed, the woman decided to take the man to court, but there are no laws that would allow her to be compensated for the damage done to her heart, the fatal blow to her self-esteem and the shame that came behind it all, so she dressed up her anger and disguised it as child support. Does she need help with her children? Sure. And this is why it's hard to confront such a woman. She'd ridicule anyone who dared to tell her that her choice to repeatedly go after that guy has everything to do with her desire to punish and control him. She'd continue to say things like, "He's not about to take care of somebody's else's children while mine are over here hungry! He helped me make them, so he needs to help me pay for them!" While this sounds admirable, it is not always as noble or maternal as it sounds. Translated, this can often be her way of saying that she's not about to watch him serve as a blessing to another woman when he'd refused to be a blessing to her. She'd become his judge and jury, and as long as she carries that unforgiveness in her heart, she will remain an enemy of what God intends to do in that man's life, thus causing her to become an enemy of what God wants to do in her life. Was the ex wrong for misleading her? Yes! Was she wrong for going outside the will of God to acquire whatever it was that he'd promised her? Yes! What she hadn't realized was that God had given her a set of boundaries to keep her heart from suffering through all of the pain it had endured, but she hadn't respected those boundaries. And when we don't take accountability for our own decisions, we set ourselves up to repeat the mistakes that broke our hearts the first time. If she learns from her lesson, takes accountability for her own actions and forgives the ex so-much-so that she chooses to co-parent with him as his sister in Christ (not his ex), she's less likely to find herself in the same situation with a different man. She'll end up married to a God-fearing man who loves her and loves her children as if they were her own. And the stories of her past will be nothing more than stories she shares with young women, teaching them to choose God's will over their own. In other words, she'll come to understand why God instituted boundaries in the first place. She'll learn to respect those boundaries and teach others to do the same.

Sometimes, I see believers who are clearly unhappy with their lives. This is evident in, not just the fact that they always appear to be upset or they are always complaining about something, but it manifests itself in their tones, their relationships and their choices. I often wonder what it is that they are playing tug-of-war with, because it's clear to me that they want something; it's almost as if they are having an extended temper tantrum at the altar. It's almost as if the altar of God is in front of them, but they won't stop clinging to what God has told them to sacrifice. In many cases, of course, the object of their unfulfilled affections is a lover who got away or a lifestyle that they haven't fully mourned yet. Respect the boundaries that God gives you. If I can, I warn these people (in love) because I know what it feels like to play tug-of-war with God. The game is fixed; the human loses and God wins—the end. But this event doesn't look like a battle between two humans because it isn't. It's a battle between the created and the Creator. God is the giver of life, so the thing that they have a death grip on suffocates in their grips. It then begins to decompose right before their eyes, and day after day, it keeps slipping through their fingers. Day after day, they pick it up again and try to ignore the altar right in front of them. Howbeit, there's something lodged in the will of the human that makes them believe that by being angry and stand-offish towards God that He'll eventually move mountains, override His own Word, and then wink one of His eyes before looking both ways. He would then silently slip them the forbidden desires of their hearts and gesture for them to remain silent about it. In other words, they've humanized God. I suspect in many of these cases that this was the type of relationship that they had with one or both of their parents or maybe a grandparent. They've learned to emotionally protest the will of God, all the while, attempting to serve Him. Their servitude may be from the heart, but it also has traces of motive in it; in other words, it's transactional. God sees this, and it is for this reason that He allows them to marinate in their bitterness year after year until they finally make a decision. "And if it seems evil unto you to serve the LORD, choose you this day whom ye will serve." God's loving voice echoes over time to respond to them, nevertheless, to them, He sounds like an unreasonable Father. So, they attempt to punish Him by complaining or sinning against Him. Of course, this behavior only backfires. This reminds me of the time when I was young, married and foolish. I don't remember what I was mad at my ex about, but I do remember sitting on the couch with my arms crossed with tears streaming down my face. The family photo of us on the coffee table in front of me only seemed to taunt me. I stared at the picture like an angry child, focusing solely on my ex and the huge smile that he had on his face—a smile that I so desperately wanted to erase in that moment. I grabbed my key chain and fumbled around with it until I had my can of mace resting in the palm of my hands. I turned the nozzle around and maced my ex's picture. It was silly (crazy even), but it was the evidence of my immaturity AND my need for deliverance. After this foolish act, I leaned back and crossed my arms once again, and then, watched as the liquid ran down the glass. *Cough.* The scent was almost unnoticeable, but the fumes were becoming increasingly unbearable. *Cough, cough.* I covered my nose hoping that I'd be able to stop coughing, but this didn't work either. It was only a matter of seconds before my nose and my eyes felt like they were on fire. I couldn't breathe, so I leaped from the seat, nearly falling into the glass table. I then ran out the living room door coughing and wheezing. How silly is that story? How silly was I? This is how so many believers behave with God. Whenever He tells them no, they do whatever they can to change His mind. In other words, they refuse to respect the boundaries that He has put in place for them. So, they sin against Him or His people in an attempt to move Him; when God addresses these behaviors, He refers to them as the people provoking Him to wrath. Every action provokes a reaction and starts a conversation that doesn't end until one or both parties submit. God's Word is final, but He can also give you over to the desires of your heart if you keep provoking Him. What does this look like? It looks like Him allowing you to have the very thing, the very person or the very lifestyle that you're willing to come against Him to get. This is called a reprobate mind!

Romans 12:21-32: Because that, when they knew God, they glorified *him* not as God, neither were thankful; but became vain in their imaginations, and their foolish heart was darkened. Professing themselves to be wise, they became fools, and changed the glory of the uncorruptible God into an image made like to corruptible man, and to birds, and fourfooted beasts, and creeping things. Wherefore God also gave them up to uncleanness through the lusts of their own hearts, to dishonour their own bodies between themselves: Who changed the truth of God into a lie, and worshipped and served the creature more than the Creator, who is blessed for ever. Amen. For this cause God gave them up unto vile affections: for even their women did change the natural use into that which is against nature: And likewise also the men, leaving the natural use of the woman, burned in their lust one toward another; men with men working that which is unseemly, and receiving in themselves that recompence of their error which was meet. And even as they did not like to retain God in their knowledge, God gave them over to a reprobate mind, to do those things which are not convenient; Being filled with all unrighteousness, fornication, wickedness, covetousness, maliciousness; full of envy, murder, debate, deceit, malignity; whisperers, Backbiters, haters of God, despiteful, proud, boasters, inventors of evil things, disobedient to parents, Without understanding, covenantbreakers, without natural affection, implacable, unmerciful: Who knowing the judgment of God, that they which commit such things are worthy of death, not only do the same, but have pleasure in them that do them.

There are people out there right now who are married to folks that God tried to protect them from. He'd drawn a boundary—a line in the sand and told them not to cross it, just as He'd done with Ahab, Solomon and all of the Israelites. Nevertheless, on the other side of His "no" stood a beautifully wrapped devil with an accent. All it needed was the person's permission to enter (and invade) their lives; in the natural, we call this permission a passport or a license. In the spirit, God calls it an agreement. "Do you take this man (or woman) to be your LAWFULLY wedded husband (or wife), to have and to hold, from this day forward, for better, for worse, for richer, for poorer, in sickness and in health, until death do us part?" The sounds of wedding bells seem to drown out the alarm sounds going off in Heaven, indicating that another boundary has been crossed. "Danger, danger!" shouts the Lord of Hosts, but the woman (or man) looks into the eyes of the weapon that was formed against her (or him) and says, "I do." Unbeknownst to them, they say these words in unison with the devil. The alarm suddenly stops as the man places the ring on the woman's finger, legalizing the warfare that Satan's about to unleash. Little does she know, she hasn't married the man, she married a principal. Little does he know, he didn't marry the woman, he married a principal.

Three years later, she finds herself looking into the eyes of the man who's attempting to strangle her, or he finds himself staring down the barrel of a loaded gun being held by the woman who legally has his surname. Those once irresistible eyes now look dark and soulless. The smile that had once captivated her (or him) is now sadistic and grimacing. Those hands that she'd allowed to cross God's boundaries to touch her outside of marriage are now hurting her, or those hands that he'd allowed to illegally touch him outside of marriage are now preparing themselves to stroke the trigger of a gun he'd purchased. As their lives begin to drain from their eyes, all of their choices flash before them. They realize, in that moment, why God said no, whether that "no" had come from the Bible, through someone else or through a sign. Nevertheless, they hadn't respected God's boundaries, so they'd ventured past them, only to find out what was on the other side of His "no." But in the nick of time, God rescues them. Nevertheless, they have to be careful. This rescuing IS NOT God's way of saying that He's going to let them have their way; it's not His way of saying that He agrees with them (many believers mistake deliverance for compliance, and they couldn't be any more further from the truth). This rescuing is God's way of extending His mercy to them, and if they dishonor God's mercy and grace in the same manner that they'd dishonored the boundaries He set in front of them, it won't be long before one or both of the individuals end up putting a wedding ring on death's middle finger.

Respecting boundaries is not always an easy feat, especially when we don't understand why they are in place. For example, whenever my Dad forbade me from having a boyfriend, I didn't fully understand his logic. It made no sense to me. In my 14-year old mind, I thought he was just being difficult, and I thought that he was going out of his way to keep me from growing up. I was reasoning like an irresponsible teen, which meant that I truly wasn't mature enough to be in a relationship, but no one would have been able to convince me of this fact at that stage of my life. So, I tried to bargain with him—I cried, I tried to get my mother to back me—I pretty much did everything I could think of to change his mind. Not long after I turned 15, my parents reached an agreement. My Dad agreed to allow me to talk over the phone with boys, but I wasn't allowed to have a boyfriend or date. He'd moved the boundaries a little, and while I was happy for the new breakthrough, I was still frustrated because I wanted to hang out with boys. Several months later, my parents split, and my mother lifted the boundaries. She allowed me to date, and almost immediately, I began to break even more boundaries, including sneaking a boyfriend in the house on occasions. Get this, we will never respect boundaries that we are not mature enough to cross. I didn't just want to date, I wanted to be grown, so lifting those boundaries didn't help me to mature; it helped me to further rebel.

Let's revisit the people who are playing tug-of-war with God. They are reasoning like the 14 and 15-year old Tiffany, the child who wanted nothing more than to stuff my future into a man's mouth and then wait on him to articulate it for her. As we discussed, God can give you a no that sounds like a yes and allow you to squeeze everything out of that experience until you come to realize that everything you need is in Him. In other words, God can allow you to have the equivalent of combination zoning, whereas, the enemy starts to live a little too close to home for you. God can allow you to have everything that you're pouting to get, but you can't just have the good of your idol, you have to accept the bad as well.

To respect boundaries doesn't just mean honoring God's Word, it also means to love God's Word. To do this, you need knowledge, you need understanding and you have to want to understand God. What I've discovered is that not everyone wants to agree with God; they simply want to rebel and comply at the same time, thinking that doing the will of God grudgingly is going to manipulate Him into giving them the desires of their ever-wicked hearts. If you want to walk with God, you have to agree with God, after all, can two walk together except they be in agreement? Let's kill the notion that we can disagree with God and walk with Him at the same time. Now, we can walk with Him and not understand the whys behind His ways, however, when we do this, we are simply walking by faith. Nevertheless, people who don't purpose in their hearts to better understand God often attempt to walk with Him and against Him at the same time. In other words, they don't respect the boundaries He's put in place for them, and when this happens, they violate those borders. Consequently, they find themselves bound.

Create boundaries in your life, and make sure that you respect your own boundaries enough to enforce them. All the same, respect the boundaries of others; this is how you surround yourself with respectable and trustworthy people. Please note that every man or woman who leaves your life simply because he or she doesn't like or agree with your boundaries is a person who God doesn't want in your life. Stop keeping people around who God is trying to drive away.

SETTING BOUNDARIES

I was talking to my Dad one day, and we were reminiscing about the past. He'd had a sudden epiphany and wanted to share it with me. With his voice trembling, he told me that he'd suddenly come to realize that he was mostly to blame for him and my Mom's divorce some 26 years earlier. I stopped him before he could go any further. Yes, they'd separated and divorced because of his wrongs, but they hadn't been a true couple for years. "Dad," I said interrupting his speech. "Both of you were to blame, not just you." I went on to tell him what I'd observed, even as a child, and why I'd been such an angry child. I saw my mother working two full time jobs and nearly collapsing anytime she walked through the door. But I also saw people, from neighbors to coworkers to family members taking advantage of her. I remember one day specifically when I was eight-years old. My Mom had just come home from her job at McRae's and she only had about an hour or two before she had to leave out for her second job. I remember her talking about how tired she was. She told me that she was going to take a nap and she wanted me to wake her up at a specific time. I agreed. But my Mom wasn't in her bedroom for long before there was a knock on the door. I didn't want to answer it. I planned to pretend that we weren't home because I knew who it was. It was our neighbor from across the street. She was a young woman, maybe in her mid-twenties, and she was always asking my Mom to take her somewhere because she didn't have a car. She lived with her grandparents, but I'm not sure why she wouldn't ask them to take her around. My Mom told me to answer the door, so I did. "Is Alice here?" I looked at the petite nuisance as she stepped over the threshold and into our living room. "She's asleep" I said, hoping she'd get the hint. But she didn't. "Can you go and wake her up, please?" I wasn't about to wake my mother up, so I didn't budge. "She's asleep," I said again, but she didn't care. "Can you go wake her up? I need to ask her something." Again, I wouldn't move. Nevertheless, my mother heard the conversation and finally came out of her room. The worrisome neighbor took her eyes off me and looked up at my mother. "Hey Alice. I need a ride. I'll give you some gas money." Lies! She was always promising my mother money for gas, but she rarely coughed it up. At first, my mother told her that she was tired and needed to rest, but the neighbor insisted (as usual). She knew how to work my mother. I don't remember the story she told, but once again, she managed to convince my mother to lose sleep just so that she wouldn't have to pay a taxi driver. "Okay. Let me get my keys," my Mom said after letting out a subtle sigh. I was so very angry with my mother, after all, I wanted her to rest. You see, my Mom was super passive, so-much-so that you won't find many people who have a negative word to speak about her. They would always say to me, for example, "Your mother is so sweet," and she was. But at the same time, she was so determined to please people that she would let just about everyone cross all over her boundaries until they were no more. This was especially true for family members.

As I recalled some of the things I'd overheard family members saying to my Mom when I was a young woman, my Dad was taken aback. "Why are you with him? You can do way better than him!" I remember hearing one relative say this, and she would repeat it just about every time she came to our house, which was often. "So, as you can see, Dad, you were both to blame. Neither one of you knew how to draw and/or enforce boundaries, and when there are no boundaries present, Satan will have a field day with your family." My Dad was silent for a moment. "You're right," he said with his voice now sounding normal again. "We just didn't know any better."

My mother passed away in October of 2018 from lung cancer. She had never been a smoker, nevertheless, smokers would often visit her and light up their cigarettes in her home. One incident happened when I was an adult, maybe around 28 or 29 years of age. I was at my mother's house curling her hair. My mother had just won her first round with cancer and I was dolling her up so that I could take some pictures of her. A woman who was close to my mother (we'll call her Jane) came over to visit. She'd known my mother since before I was born, so we saw her as a part of our family. As Jane made her way into the den, she placed a cigarette in her mouth and prepared to light it. "Don't light that cigarette in this house," I said interrupting her. My mother kept quiet, but Jane immediately became aggravated. "This ain't your house!" she shouted. She then yelled about how she was going to smoke her cigarette and how I didn't tell her what to do. I calmly repeated myself a few more times. "Don't light that cigarette in this house." I continued to curl my mother's hair despite Jane's outrage. She let out a few more profane words and then grabbed her cigarette lighter, but not before questioning my mother. "Alice, are you gonna let her stand there and talk to me like that? Alice?!" My Mom didn't say a word. At this point in her life, she appreciated the fact that I enforced the boundaries that she had established long ago, but had never enforced. This was because my mother hated confrontation and she didn't like to offend people out of fear that they'd walk out of her life and never look back. What she feared, I desired. In other words, I wanted toxic people to leave my life, so I picked up the can of hairspray and pointed it in her direction. "Okay," I said calmly. "Go ahead and light it. Light it and watch me light you up." Jane had just flicked her cigarette lighter and was ready to light her cigarette before I issued the threat, but she removed her hand from the lighter's clicker and stared at me for a few seconds. She looked for fear in my eyes, but it wasn't there. Suddenly, she broke her silence. "That's why I don't come over here!" she yelled, making her way towards the living room and storming out the door. "You've always been disrespectful!" she shouted. She kept yelling out a bunch of inaudible words as she exited my mother's house, but I didn't care. Again, I didn't share her fears because I'd seen the damage done to my mother's life by keeping toxic people around, so I wanted them to walk away. I remember this story because of the comical end of it. When Jane went outside, she found my mother's then live-in boyfriend and one of our relatives standing outside smoking their cigarettes as well. "She put you out too?" one of the men snickered as he looked at Jane. On that day, three people were at my mother's house lighting up their cigarettes, and I'd put them all outside because she wouldn't do it. In that moment, I was drawing a line of demarcation around my mother, but little did I know, it was too late. My mother would fight many types of cancers over the next ten years, and would eventually succumb to lung cancer. But my mother didn't die from cancer, despite what the doctors say. She left this Earth at the tender age of 61 because she had never come to know her worth. Her cause of death? Lack of boundaries.

As I mentioned earlier, one of my greatest fears was becoming like my mother. Don't get me wrong; she had many traits and qualities that I'm honored to carry, but her gift of charity was a gift that I didn't want. Nevertheless, I inherited it. I didn't initially realize that the gift of charity is a blessing, but it only becomes problematic when it's not paired with wisdom, discernment and boundaries. Think of it this way—any gift that God gives you is like a precious jewel. It's beautiful, it's valuable and it's on high demand. To protect it, you must draw boundaries around it. A jeweler will always place his most valuable gems behind a locked glass counter. Also, behind that counter, you'll likely find several guns. This is because the jeweler recognizes the fact that buyers and potential buyers aren't the only ones attracted to what he has to offer; thieves are also attracted to the gems. Nevertheless, the thief has no desire to polish and feature the gems for others to see; his desire is to steal as much as he can and sell what he's stolen on the black market. To protect his investment from thieves, the jeweler has to have a pretty stable security system, complete with a video surveillance, weapons, locks and maybe even a security guard. The more security you see around a particular gem, the more valuable it is. Why don't we understand this as it relates to ourselves? If I truly believe that I'm valuable, I'll have standards that will drive most men away. This isn't bad; it's good! My goal is to drive away any and everyone who doesn't understand or respect my value, but to get to this place, I had to first learn my own value, and then come to respect it. The same is true for you. Sure, you may have found yourself dating one narcissist after the next and befriending a bunch of narcissists, and while it is easy to point out the wicked things they've done to you, your freedom won't come until you take accountability for what happened to the adult-sized you. What does this mean? It's simple. You didn't do what God told you to do; you didn't guard your heart. It doesn't matter if the narcissist love-bombed you, the fact still remains that you allowed yourself to be love-bombed. If you don't come to this conclusion, you'll keep dating the same demon in a different body. This is because you'll keep pointing at the weeds that are growing in your garden, rather than pointing at the seeds that you planted in that garden. I call this the maintenance effect. Think of a yard. A woman complains that weeds keep growing in her yard, so to make her lawn look better, she repeatedly hires a lawn company to cut her grass. While this makes the lawn look better, within a matter of days, those weeds will become noticeable again. To rid her yard of weeds, she has to deal with the root of the issue. She can't put more of her focus on what's growing in her yard than she puts on why it's growing in her yard. The why explains the what! To truly make her yard a beautiful one, she has to put down some weed killer, and every time she finds a weed growing, she has to pull it up by the root. All the same, to keep her yard weed-free, she has to set boundaries. The same is true for you.

Setting boundaries first starts with you cleaning out your life. You have to remove the weeds if you want to remove the wild animals. If I allow my backyard to become a forest, I have allowed it to become a habitation for wild animals. Now, I can have all the animals removed, but it's only a matter of time before the insects and the four-legged beasts return. This is because wild animals live in the wilderness. What this means is, I can't complain about what lives in my backyard until I address the state of my backyard! I would have to cut down some trees, keep the grass moved, prune whatever I'm growing and monitor the space daily. I could have trees and plants; they would just need to be in order. And understand this—wherever there are trees and plants, animals will inevitably come. My goal is to draw boundaries around my property to keep them out. I'd erect a fence and spray my garden with pesticides. I'd set up cameras around my property and I'd make sure that I frequented the space so that I could monitor it. The question then remains—how do I drive the wild animals out of my life? The word "no" is one of the most powerful words that you possess in your vocabulary. Use words like "no" and "don't." For example, establish boundaries in your life, especially in the areas where you've suffered the most heartache or damage. Communicate your boundaries to the people in your life, and do not be afraid of their faces or their responses! Bound people hate boundaries; I can't emphasize that enough! And they love to gaslight and cast themselves as the victims whenever they realize that their mind games are coming to an abrupt end. Don't be afraid to lose them! The problem with most people is—they try to hold onto people that God is trying to deliver them from! Narcissists are skilled at making themselves appear to be important, needed and valuable structures in the lives of the people they are manipulating. Stop lying to yourself! You see what you see, you feel what you feel and you've experienced what you've experienced—it's all real and you're not crazy! You were simply gaslighted. It's okay. Many of us have been taken advantage of at some point, especially those of us who are empathetic (prophetic) and/or have the gift of charity. But remember, you need the gift of discernment, wisdom and boundaries to guard this gift! Otherwise, you'll be like a jewelry store with no surveillance or locks. You'd be constantly robbed of your peace and everything that's valuable to you.

Howbeit, you need clear and concise instructions, right? There's nothing wrong with that! Below, I've listed the steps to setting healthy boundaries around yourself, and a few steps to enforcing these boundaries.

1. Devils can't be domesticated. What this means is, try as you may, you can't talk a devil out of being evil, after all, the word "evil" is found in the word "devil." In other words, stop trying to change people who love being toxic. Come to realize that they get to choose the lives and the lifestyles that they want, just like you get to choose what you want your life to look like. Stop thinking that you have their best interests in mind and do what you need to do to get your healing. Whenever and if ever they should decide to heal, that's a journey that they have to take independent of your influence.

2. Write the vision and make it plain. Take some time out of your day for the next few days and write down some of the issues that you've had to endure over the course of your life, especially the last five years. After you're done, establish rules to prevent these things from happening again. For example, my new rules are (1). I will not have sex before marriage. (2). I will not unequally yoke myself with an unbeliever. (3). I will be accountable to someone wiser than myself whenever I am courting someone. I will not be afraid to allow another person to examine the individual who's pursuing me and give me advice and instructions regarding the guy and/or the relationship.

3. Get deliverance. If you're not familiar with the ministry of deliverance, look it up. If you don't agree with the

doctrine of deliverance, study Mark 16:17, Matthew 10:1, James 4:7, and Mark 16:17. If your church doesn't minister deliverance, simply find a credible ministry in your area to get deliverance or go to a deliverance conference. Believers should receive deliverance every quarter or, at minimum, twice a year.

4. Get counseling. Therapy is one of the most underrated but mostly needed events that most people take for granted. This helps you to deal with the roots of many of the issues and choices you've suffered through.

5. Surround yourself with emotionally healthy people. You do this by not tolerating toxic people and then getting the healing you need to become what you want to attract to yourself.

6. Change your phone number! To rid yourself of toxic people, you need a fresh start! Don't just block their numbers, completely cut all access off to you by changing your number!

7. Stop following them on social media. Sometimes, the issue is that you just won't let go of the car that's dragging you.

8. If the toxic person is a family member, create a standard of communication. For example, your published boundaries should read like, "I will not tolerate anyone calling me out of my name, yelling at me, gaslighting me or using any other methods of manipulation to control me." Communicate your new

rules to your loved ones in a neutral place, for example, invite your mother, father, sibling, niece, nephew, aunt or uncle out to lunch. Be kind and have a great time. While there, let them know that you have been doing some soul-searching and you've decided that from here on out, you want to have a healthy relationship with them and every person in your life. After that, take accountability for all of the toxic things you have a tendency of doing, and then, verbally commit to not doing them anymore. Lastly, show the person your published rules. You can say, this is my new "life contract." Of course, the person will feel targeted and look confused. Don't be passive-aggressive. Be direct and answer any questions that he or she may have, reminding the person that you are just as guilty as he or she is. All the same, let the individual know that you're communicating your new boundaries to everyone who you see as a valuable fixture in your life; this way, you can potentially preserve those relationships. Please understand that this may be an incredibly uncomfortable conversation, but it's a necessary one.

9. Enforce your boundaries. This means that after the meeting with the relative, should he or she violate your boundaries, warn the person (in love). For example, if a relative of mine started shouting over the phone, I'd warn him or her in one of two ways. I'd either tell the person to lower his or her voice, reminding the individual that we can communicate in

a healthy manner or I'd hang up the phone. If the person calls me back, I may answer the first time just to see if he or she has calmed down. If not, I'd disconnect the line again. After this, I'd either cut off all communication with the person or limit his or her access to me. Again, this is important—this is NOT done to punish the individual at all! The goal is to draw and enforce boundaries, helping the individual to understand that having a toxic relationship with you is not an option!

10. Forgive yourself. The establishing of boundaries can be relatively devasting at first because many of the people you love and have grown accustomed to will see themselves as victims or they'll pretend to see themselves as victims. Consequently, they'll walk out of your life. Many of them are not fully trying to disconnect from you; they are simply attempting to punish and train you. The options that they are giving you are to either (a) have a toxic relationship with them or (b) lose access to them. Always choose option b.

11. Heal. Again, get yourself a therapist and educate yourself about narcissism, the Jezebel spirit, toxic relationships and so on. Healing is not a product of time; it is a product of intention. In other words, you have to study your way out of pain.

12. Keep God first at all times. He is the skin we need to protect us from the many viruses like narcissists. If you put Him first, Satan won't have any place in your

life.

Again, setting boundaries is not always something fun to do, but it's necessary. All the same, you will soon come to understand why so many people who've come out of toxic families or have extensive histories with toxic people have escaped their narcissistic pharaohs and never looked back. This is because they found peace, and whenever a human enters into something as tangible and as supernatural as peace, that person will likely never tolerate another toxic person!

A NOTE TO THE EMPATH AND THE PROPHETIC INDIVIDUAL

Idolatry. It's the spiritual equivalent of adultery and, of course, adultery is the natural equivalent of idolatry. To be idolatrous simply means to put something or someone before God; it means to reverence, exalt or worship someone or something over the Most High God Himself (YAHWEH). But worship doesn't always look like people getting down on their knees and bowing down; sometimes, worship looks like sex outside of marriage. "Therefore I urge you, brethren, by the mercies of God, to present your bodies a living and holy sacrifice, acceptable to God, which is your spiritual service of worship" (Romans 12:1). Sometimes, worship looks like unequally yoking yourself with an unbeliever. Sometimes, worship looks like you buying tickets to go and support your favorite celebrities, but getting mad when your pastor starts talking about tithes and offerings. Whatever you worship, you will submit to, whether it's submitting your body, your funds or the direction of your life. Believe it or not, it is easy for the prophetic person, also known as the empath, to fall into the snares of idolatry. It's equally as easy for them to fall into the snares of adultery. Again, this is because prophetic people are wired to be sensitive, some more than others. So, prophetic people have to be more careful at guarding their hearts than most people; that is, until they've matured and given God His rightful place in their hearts. But maturity is a product of understanding, not time. This is important to note because there are a lot of immature believers who've been saved for twenty plus years! And many of them believe themselves to be mature when they are not, and this can be seen in their choices, who they surround themselves with and what they are consistently drawn to. And of all the rejected, abused, abandoned and mismanaged empaths/prophetic people I've counseled, I can truly say without doubt or question that, as empathic/prophetic individuals, we are the biggest problems in our own equations. This is because the easiest trap for an empath to fall into is the snare of idolatry. And when an empath falls into idolatry, an Ahab is born.

Narc. #1	Narc. #2	Narc. #3	Narc. #4	Narc. #5	Narc. #6
Self	Self	Self	Self	Self	Self

What you can see from the fraction above is that you (self) are the common denominator in every failed or toxic relationship that you've entered. This should speak volumes to you. But there's more to this problem than meets the eye. This isn't to say that you CAUSE the problems in the relationship; it is to say that the problem is the relationship itself! What's missing from the equation? Or better yet, who is missing from the equation? The obvious answer is—God! But for believers, God isn't necessarily absent from their lives, He's just not number one in their lives, and this is blatant idolatry! Most believers reason that as long as they're Christian and God is somewhere in their hearts (or plans) that everything else should fall into place, but this is deception at its best! Matthew 6:33 instructs (or warns) us this way, "But seek ye **first** the kingdom of God, and his righteousness; and all these things shall be added unto you." Notice that the scripture said to seek the Kingdom of God FIRST! This is an ordinance, meaning, it deals primarily with legalities and order. This is where most of us have failed. We're seeking the Kingdom, just not first. And get this—going to church, joining a ministry, singing in the choir, hosting Bible study or running twelve laps around a church is NOT seeking the Kingdom! It's serving the Kingdom, and in some cases, it can be self-serving, depending on your motives. Seeking God first means putting your plans off so that you can get to know Him better. Serving God means replacing your plans for you with His plans for you. Putting Him first allows Him to be our leader, meaning, we'll follow His will and His directions for our lives. Please note that you will ALWAYS be led by whatever it is that you put first! 2 Timothy 3:1-7 states, "This know also, that in the last days perilous times shall come. For men shall be lovers of their own selves, covetous, boasters, proud, blasphemers, disobedient to parents, unthankful, unholy, without natural affection, trucebreakers, false accusers, incontinent, fierce, despisers of those that are good, traitors, heady, highminded, lovers of pleasures more than lovers of God; Having a form of godliness, but denying the power thereof: from such turn away. For of this sort are they which creep into houses, and lead captive silly women laden with sins, led away with divers lusts, ever learning, and never able to come to the knowledge of the truth." Why are men lovers of themselves these days? Because they put themselves first! Why are silly women led astray by these men? Because they've put themselves or their lovers first! Again, whatever you put first will be what you're led by; yes, even if you are Christian, you love the Lord and you are called according to His purpose! God absolutely has to be number one in our lives; any other arrangement is idolatrous. Look at the Empathic Equation below.

The Prophetic Equation #1					
Narc. #1	Narc. #2	Narc. #3	Narc. #4	Narc. #5	Narc. #6
RELIGION	**RELIGION**	**RELIGION**	**RELIGION**	**RELIGION**	**RELIGION**
SELF	SELF	SELF	SELF	SELF	SELF

You'll notice that the Prophetic Equation suggests that the empaths or prophetic people on this spectrum tend to put their lovers before God. Nevertheless, in many of these cases, they appear to put God before themselves, but this is still idolatry, and it always leads to heartbreak, disappointment and a host of other issues. Please note that Prophetic Equation #1 is a works mentality; it is to be law-minded, instead of faith-focused. What this means is:

1. Empaths in this equation appear to place God above themselves, but this is just a mirage. It's religiousness camouflaged by Christian works. It means to have the appearance of Godliness, but deny the power thereof. In all truth, anytime you place another human above God, it's because you've erected yourself and your

274

own desires about the will of God.

2. The (Christian) empath tries to overcompensate for his/her own idolatry by "performing" for God. This is similar to a man committing adultery against his wife, but coming home every day with roses and attempting to put on his best sexual performance, even though his virtue has been hijacked by the other woman. Consequently, what he does with his wife is more rhythmic than it is intimate. This is the very "expression" of religion!

3. Empaths on this spectrum demonstrate the hands of God (works), but not the heart of God (faith).

The Prophetic Equation #2					
Narc. #1	Narc. #2	Narc. #3	Narc. #4	Narc. #5	Narc. #6
SELF	SELF	SELF	SELF	SELF	SELF
RELIGION	**RELIGION**	**RELIGION**	**RELIGION**	**RELIGION**	**RELIGION**

In Prophetic Equation #2, you'll notice that the (Ahab'ed) empath places his or her lover above himself/herself, but the empath places himself/herself before God. In all truth, this equation is a more accurate depiction of what it means to be bound by the Ahab spirit. Again, this is religiousness, which is why you'll notice that God is nowhere in the aforementioned equations.

The Narcissistic Equation #1					
SELF	SELF	SELF	SELF	SELF	SELF
RELIGION	**RELIGION**	**RELIGION**	**RELIGION**	**RELIGION**	**RELIGION**

Emp. #1	Emp. #2	Emp. #3	Emp. #4	Emp. #5	Emp. #6

The Narcissistic Equation #2					
RELIGION	RELIGION	RELIGION	RELIGION	RELIGION	RELIGION
SELF	SELF	SELF	SELF	SELF	SELF
Emp. #1	Emp. #2	Emp. #3	Emp. #4	Emp. #5	Emp. #6

The narcissist (Jezebel spirit) will always place himself/herself above others and before God. Remember that Jezebel in the Bible was an idol worshiper. So, what we can gather from the aforementioned equations is that both the Ahab'ed empaths and the narcissists have placed themselves, their needs and their desires above the will of God, but they can and will serve religion. Serving religion or being religious is not the same thing as serving God; it's performance-based. And please note that being an empath is NOT necessarily the same as being bound by the Ahab spirit. In these equations, I'm dealing with empaths who are bound by this spirit. To be empathic means to be prophetic, but if your prophetic wiring is hijacked by the narcissist, you will need deliverance from the Ahab spirit. Let's look at God's original design.

Godhead
You
Others

Note: the listing above is in no way suggesting that you

place your needs above the needs of others; it simply means that you have to remove the plank from your own eyes before you attempt to help anyone else. It means to lead by example. When the proper ordinances of God are established in our lives, we will be cured of the disease that is the narcissist! Again, this is all about ORDER! 1 Corinthians 11:2-3 speaks of Godly order; it reads, "Now I praise you, brethren, that ye remember me in all things, and keep the ordinances, as I delivered them to you. But I would have you know, that the head of every man is Christ; and the head of the woman is the man; and the head of Christ is God."

God
Christ
Holy Spirit
Man
Wife

Again, this deals with order! It is the cure for idolatry and every other issue on the face of this planet! Giving God His proper place is no easy feat, especially for those of us who were brought up in idolatrous households. Our wrestling matches with idolatry are almost always extensive and dramatic. And like many of our predecessors, we can defeat the golden calves in our lives and finally give God back His proper seat in our hearts if we are willing to put God's will before our own. "And I, if I be lifted up from the earth, will draw all men unto me" (John 12:32).

The God Equation					
YAHWEH	YAHWEH	YAHWEH	YAHWEH	YAHWEH	YAHWEH
SELF	SELF	SELF	SELF	SELF	SELF
Others	Others	Others	Others	Others	Others

In the God Equation, God takes His proper seat in our lives; this is because we've placed everything and everyone else in order. And get this—when you establish order in your life, there will be some people who will walk out of your life. Why? Because they weren't supposed to be there in the first place. It can also be because you gave them a measure of access to your heart that they were not mature, healed or loving enough to have. It's important that you know this because I don't want you to romanticize what establishing and enforcing boundaries is going to look like. I want to give you a realistic view of this event. When you establish order and put God first, narcissistic people will berate you, accuse you of being controlling, high-minded, religious, fake or whatever labels they can conjure up. This is designed to get you to question your heart, motives and your choices; this way, the narcissist can continue operating in your life without detection or interruption. But the minute a narcissist realizes that he or she is about to be ejected or rejected from your life, that narcissist will start using whatever tools and wiles he or she can find to bring you back into submission. If and when this doesn't work, the narcissist will then look for ways to humiliate you, destroy your reputation, destroy your career, destroy your relationships or bring destruction to anything that you value. This is the narcissist's last attempt to prove to you that they are all-powerful in your life. But make no mistake about it. The war isn't truly against you; their war is with God. Ephesians 6:12 confirms this. It reads, "For we wrestle not against flesh and blood, but against principalities, against powers, against the rulers of the darkness of this world, against spiritual wickedness in high places." This is just an extension of the war that took place in Heaven. Revelation 12:1-9 summarizes this event. It reads, "And there appeared a great wonder in heaven; a woman clothed with the sun, and the moon under her feet, and upon her head a crown of twelve stars: And she being with child cried, travailing in birth, and pained to be delivered.

And there appeared another wonder in heaven; and behold a great red dragon, having seven heads and ten horns, and seven crowns upon his heads. And his tail drew the third part of the stars of heaven, and did cast them to the earth: and the dragon stood before the woman which was ready to be delivered, for to devour her child as soon as it was born. And she brought forth a man child, who was to rule all nations with a rod of iron: and her child was caught up unto God, and to his throne. And the woman fled into the wilderness, where she hath a place prepared of God, that they should feed her there a thousand two hundred and threescore days. And there was war in heaven: Michael and his angels fought against the dragon; and the dragon fought and his angels, and prevailed not; neither was their place found any more in heaven. And the great dragon was cast out, that old serpent, called the Devil, and Satan, which deceiveth the whole world: he was cast out into the earth, and his angels were cast out with him." The dragon, of course, is Satan. The man child who was and is to rule all nations is Jesus Christ. Satan and his angels (demons) waged war against God, but we know how that ended. They lost. Now, we don't war with the enemy since the war has already been won; instead, we engage in warfare. The battleground is our minds, but please be reminded that warfare doesn't always look like bloodshed and chaos. Sometimes, it's a thought or an imagination. Sometimes, it's romantic. Sometimes, it looks like a great financial opportunity. Sometimes, it's a "hello" from a beautiful stranger. To Samson, warfare came through a beautifully decorated seductress called Delilah. To Uriah, warfare looked like a promotion from the king. To Tamar, deception looked like her father telling her to go and care for her ailing brother; in other words, it looked like trust and affirmation. Of course, David didn't deceive her, Amnon did. To the unnamed prophet mentioned in 1 Kings 13, warfare looked like another prophet giving him a false prophecy that would cost him his life! The point is, Satan doesn't always engage us in outright warfare. Sometimes, he simply deceives us. But when God has His proper place in our hearts and in our lives, Satan is then rendered powerless. This is why he gauges us to see what it is that we want; this way, he can use that thing or that person as bait. He then engages our imaginations, using them as big screens where he then plays the infomercials of what we could potentially have. To defeat this tactic, God told us in 2 Corinthians 10:5,

"Casting down imaginations, and every high thing that exalteth itself against the knowledge of God, and bringing into captivity every thought to the obedience of Christ." He "cast" Satan and his angels out of Heaven, and now, He tells us to "cast" down the imaginations that rise up against His will for our lives, even when those imaginations are pleasant. One rule of thumb to consider is this—whatever we don't cast down will ultimately have to be cast out. What this means is warfare starts with temptation, but demonic oppression starts the minute the believer gives into that temptation. This means that the believer becomes a prisoner of war. What does this look like? Again, consider the plight of Samson. Judges 16:15-21 reads, "And she said unto him, How canst thou say, I love thee, when thine heart is not with me? Thou hast mocked me these three times, and hast not told me wherein thy great strength lieth. And it came to pass, when she pressed him daily with her words, and urged him, so that his soul was vexed unto death; that he told her all his heart, and said unto her, There hath not come a razor upon mine head; for I have been a Nazarite unto God from my mother's womb: if I be shaven, then my strength will go from me, and I shall become weak, and be like any other man. And when Delilah saw that he had told her all his heart, she sent and called for the lords of the Philistines, saying, Come up this once, for he hath shewed me all his heart. Then the lords of the Philistines came up unto her, and brought money in their hand. And she made him sleep upon her knees; and she called for a man, and she caused him to shave off the seven locks of his head; and she began to afflict him, and his strength went from him. And she said, The Philistines be upon thee, Samson. And he awoke out of his sleep, and said, I will go out as at other times before, and shake myself. And he wist not that the LORD was departed from him. But the Philistines took him, and put out his eyes, and brought him down to Gaza, and bound him with fetters of brass; and he did grind in the prison house."

Again, what does a prisoner of war look like?

1. **They are deceived.** Samson was a prisoner of the narcissistic Delilah before he became a prisoner of the Philistines.
2. **They are vexed.** The scripture tells us that Delilah vexed Samson to death with her nagging.
3. **They have relinquished their authority.** Samson laid his head (authority) on the lap (lower parts) of Delilah. Why? Because the Bible says that she "made him to sleep." Women know how to put men to sleep. Biblically speaking, he gave his strength to a woman (see Proverbs 31:3).
4. **They are confused.** Can you imagine how difficult it must have been for Samson, knowing on one hand that the woman he was with was not only forbidden by God, but also knowing that there was a possibility that she was trying to destroy him? Don't think for one second that Samson didn't consider this, but like most prophets and prophetic people who've been Ahab'ed by a narcissist, he simply wanted to believe otherwise or, at minimum, he thought he could change her mind.

5. **They are bound.** Delilah bound Samson with a soul tie before the Philistines were able to bind him in chains and fetters.

6. **They are blind.** The truth dances in their faces, but they can't see it OR they choose to ignore it. To capture Samson, the enemy gauged him and saw that he had a problem with women, the enemy engaged him by sending Delilah his way, and then, the enemy gouged out his eyes. This is the ultimate goal of the enemy when he comes across a prophet, prophetic person or a seer. To remove the eyes means to disrupt the communication between God and the prophet or prophetic person; it means to remove the prophetic person's ability to see the truth.

And remember, all of this is a DIRECT RESULT of the empath putting himself, herself or the empath's lover before God! Godly order is designed to protect you, your God-given assignment, your mind, your peace and your relationship with God! There are so many believers out there today who have not heard from God for a long time, even though they are prophetic, and this is because they have placed someone or something in God's seat of authority in their lives. Consequently, they are slowly robbed of their peace, their ability to see prophetically, their ability to hear prophetically and their ability to speak prophetically. But like Samson, their hair (abilities) can and does grow back; that is, if they don't constantly keep putting their heads (authority) on the lap of a desolate woman or man. Please understand that you don't possess the power, the tools or the abilities to make a broken person love you! There is absolutely NOTHING that Samson could have done to get Delilah to love him. She was narcissistic and Godless, so his relationship with her was pointless (at least, to the Kingdom) and illegal. But to the devil, their relationship did have a point (objective) and that was to bring Samson into captivity.

I said all of that to say this—you have a call on your life—answer it! Despite what you feel, want, hear and see, you were not designed and placed here in the Earth realm to get married, have babies and die. Sure, getting married and having children may be a part of God's plan for you, but this isn't His ultimate plan or the full picture. In other words, you may have given that fantasy a greater place in your heart than it should have. This is why God told us to cast down imaginations and every high thing that exalts itself against the knowledge of God. When the Bible refers to a "high thing," it's referring to an idol. What God is saying is to remove its value, or another way to say it is, to give Him greater value in your life. You do this by chasing Him, studying His Word, being prayerful and consciously and continuously making the choice to put Him above yourself and others! This has to be a decision you make every single day of your life, especially if you are prophetic! Note: everyone who has the Holy Spirit is prophetic, but this does NOT make them a prophet. All the same, there are degrees or levels of prophetic abilities; in other words, some people are more prophetic than others which, of course, would cause them to be more sensitive than others. And extremely sensitive or prophetic people NEED to have an apostle somewhere in their lives! Apostles are not wired to be sensitive; instead, they are wired for war. If you don't have an Apostle or an apostolic person to lead or mentor you, chances are, you may find yourself under the power and influence of a narcissist (Jezebel). Also, please note that not everyone who claims to be an apostle is an apostle; there are false apostles, just as there are false prophets. The way to distinguish the two is through prayer, studying the Word, and lastly, by being patient and sober enough to look for the fruit that springs up in their lives.

In closing, give God back His seat in your life. This is how you rid yourself of the narcissist's influence. I see men and women all over social media bragging about having gotten free from a narcissist, but most of them don't realize that they have to break up with the mindset that agrees with and invites the narcissist into their lives, and they have to divorce the Jezebel spirit. And because they don't know this, it's only a matter of time before many of them find themselves in another toxic relationship with a covert or overt narcissist. Eventually, many believers who do this grow bitter and distrusting. Many even begin to isolate themselves in an attempt to protect and hide themselves from narcissistic people. This is not the answer, nor is it the cure. The cure is ORDER! Order cuts off the head of idolatry!

Child of God, you have purpose! Yes, even those of you who

are not saved! God is calling you back to Himself so that He can use you. He wired you the way that you've been wired so that He can use you for His glory! This is your identity! If you've been trying to figure out who you are, your answer is right here. You are a product of God's imagination, but He didn't cast you down, He birthed you for such a time as this! And maybe, you grew up in a home where idolatry was prevalent, perversion was normal and love was lacking, and consequently, you went on a journey to find yourself. You were looking for the voice that Satan stole from you before you entered the Earth. You were looking for your identity; you were looking to find a place where you could feel normal since you've always stood out. God didn't wire you to be normal; He designed you to stand out, but even in standing out, there are people out there like you who you can fit in with. This is why you should join a prophetic community; this will allow you to further understand yourself, your wiring and why you were created. This will also help you to get the training you need to properly and healthily exercise your gifting. Please know this—you were designed to care! This is why you keep trying to fix broken folks! You can't do this, especially if you are engaging them romantically. You have to get into a good church where you can get the healing and tools you'll need to safely and effectively help those who are broken, but more so, those who GENUINELY want to be helped. Some people don't want your help, they just want your attention, and if getting your attention means that they have to cast themselves as victims, they'll do just that! From there, they will proceed to make you their victim. Push past every wind of doctrine, temptation and obstacle that gets in your way. When you embrace your true identity and begin to walk in it, you will fill those voids in your life. Push past the temptation to quit and make sure that you establish and enforce solid boundaries around yourself. If someone exits your life because of these boundaries, that person is bound and should not be there; I don't care what religious titles they hold!

Be sure to reread this book over and over again until the information in it starts sticking to your mind. When this happens, it will change how you respond to life, narcissists and temptation. Once you are aware of your wiring and how the enemy hijacks that wiring, you soon learn how to effectively and strategically resist the enemy and his henchmen. You've got this because God's got you! Are you ready to step into place and finally see the world from God's perspective? Let's grow! Study the Word of God every single day of your life and don't give your brain a break from Him (the Word). Getting to know Him is the same as getting to know yourself because you will see who you are in His reflection! Now go and build those boundaries!

www.ingramcontent.com/pod-product-compliance
Lightning Source LLC
Chambersburg PA
CBHW072339090426
42741CB00012B/2843